Dog Professional's Survival Guide

Sally Gutteridge

Copyright

No part of this book may be reproduced in any form - written, electronic, recording, or photocopying without written permission of the publisher or author. The exception would be in the case of brief quotations embodied in the critical articles or reviews and pages where permission is specifically granted by the author.

Although every precaution has been taken to verify the accuracy of the information contained herein, the author and publisher assume no responsibility for any errors or omissions. No liability is assumed for damages that may result from the use of information contained within.

Interior Layout: Sandeep Likhar
Editor: Beverley Boorer
Illustrator: Dayle Smith

Books may be purchased by contacting the publisher and author at:
info@sallygutteridge.com
www.sallygutteridge.com

Imprint: Independently published

© 2018 by Sally Gutteridge.
All rights reserved.

Table of Contents

Author Note 5

Introduction..6

Chapter One: Life On Earth 7
    The Rules 10
    Courage 12
    The Comfort Zone 14

Chapter Two: Finding Your Path 17
    Energy 21
    Entrainment 23
    The Beauty Of Ideas...25
    Money...26

Chapter Three: Think Carefully.......................................29
    Mindfulness 38
    The Three Principles..42
    The Magic Moment..45
    Changing Your Brain...49

Chapter Four: Life With A Wild Mind 54
    Depression...55
    Stress..59
    Anxiety 65
    Compassion Fatigue..66

Chapter Five: Resilience 71
    Habits Of Resilient People 71
    Becoming Resilient..75

Chapter Six – People: The Ultimate Test 96

    The Nature Of Defence 97
    The Blame Game 103
    Emotional Intelligence. 105
    Connection 109
    Conflict Resolution 114

Chapter Seven: Your Professional Presence 117

    The Internet 117
    Continued Professional Development 124
    Making It Pay 126
    Your Ultimate Success 130
    Final Note 132

Author Note

Every book that I write is needed somewhere in the dog world, but none more than this one. It came to me in a flash of inspiration, into a blank mind, from your energy out there in the world and is written for you. If you're reading my words as a dog professional on any level, you know the trials of the role. It's those and your ultimate success that we are addressing here.

Throughout the book we will work with a series of mind models that when learned and practiced can change your experience of life on earth.

I hope you enjoy it and benefit greatly, thank you for reading.

Introduction

I suspect you always wanted to work with dogs? Maybe you created an agility course in your grandparents' garden and had your delighted family dog jumping over poles even before you reached double figures? Perhaps you grew up in the middle of a town, or within a low-income family and working with dogs seemed out of reach, so you had to work in retail or an office instead, then suddenly twenty years have passed whilst you glanced away.

Or maybe you do work with dogs but find it a hard slog. Perhaps the income is low, you struggle with the exact role you're in or your self-belief is shattered. Or perhaps you're making an excellent job of growing a successful small business but there's something missing. You don't feel like you thought you would when this was a dream and you don't know where to go next.

Whatever your situation is, I'm writing this for you. Whether you're at the beginning of your journey, scared of taking that first step or simply worn down by years of rescuing, this is for you.

Chapter One
Life on Earth

"Doing is a quantum leap from imagining" - Barbara Sher

Ask yourself what life on earth means to you. Take a few moments right now and write it down or say it out loud in a sentence, then carry on reading.

Great, thanks! Now I bet your sentence matches the physical life you are in right now. If you think life's scary, it's likely that scary things have happened to you, so you tread carefully. If your opinion of life on earth is that it's a fun adventure, I suspect you try new things regularly and laugh a lot. If you consider life on earth to be a boring struggle, I bet your days of toil blend seamlessly from one to the next, extinguishing any briefly inspired spark that you experience.

I'm going to ask you to suspend reality during this chapter. I want you to question everything you believe to be real and form a new world for yourself. We are going to swing as far away from science as it's possible to go and then back again, to theories that open your heart and mind to your chosen future and empower you to follow your imagination into the solid form of reality.

What does this have to do with working with dogs, I can hear you thinking it. Well not exactly, but it is what I would be thinking right now, so needs acknowledging just in case.

The answer is: everything!

Every single thing begins in your mind, inclusive of a successful business, a written book, a supportive and kind environment and a whole host of clients. Moving from that crappy office job that fills your heart with dread, into a career as a canine coach begins in your mind. Passing that dog behaviour degree with flying colours, or finding that perfect home for your complex foster dog all starts with the seed of an idea, an inspiration or the choice to take a chance.

Life on earth can be your adventure, it can be your subjective reality or a lucid dream. We don't know where we are from or where we are going afterwards. We have no proof of either, we don't even know whether our consciousness will survive outside our physical body. Even after lots of exploration and tons of presented theories, we still don't know a fraction of the secrets that this beautiful universe holds. And here's a mind-blowing fact, we don't even know how many universes there are.

Let's consider for a moment that you have been living an uninspiring life for the past ten years. You might sell your time by the hour to work hard on someone else's business, helping them to chase their dreams. You may even have ethical concerns about the nature of your day job but are not able to see a way out. So, for all these years, you have wished your life away, scared to take a chance on change and hoping to win the lottery.

Now, imagine that you are not actually in a physical world at all, but an elaborate, lucid dreaming pod. You are lying there suspended in air, not going anywhere, and only your consciousness is living this life. Like Neo in The Matrix; which I highly recommend watching if you haven't already or watching again if you have. Imagine that to change the world you live in now, you only need to change it in your mind and that has been the case all along.

If this was the case and you only needed to take your mind in a different direction, for your life to go in that direction too, what would you do? Would you take the red pill as Neo did and explore it, or would you take the safe way to prevent insecurity and stay exactly where you're at? Notice that I didn't say prevent something awful from happening, to stop you losing your home or giving up everything you care about?

That was on purpose because the only thing that stops most people from taking their life in a different direction, is the possibility of it not working out. Imagine that; just a possibility of it not working out. You might not be following your dreams, *just in case it doesn't work out*.

The Rules

Life on earth, well certainly the one we inhabit in the Western World is dictated by rules. Each rule falls apart when we look closely at it. But we learned them when we were very young, so they are pretty much established. For example, we get good grades, we get a degree in something or other, a job with a good company that pays well, meet a suitably attractive spouse, have kids, put them through school then work until we can afford a few years retirement – then we die. Each step along the way is considered a successful one by the rules of society. It's a blueprint for life as a human. But whose rules are they? They are certainly not mine and if you ask yourself honestly, can you say hand on heart that they are yours?

Let's take a look at one of these rules that's close to my heart and the point I'm making. The idea that we must have a good job with a respected organisation to be successful. A second assumption about this idea is that we are much more secure with a wage or salary coming in from one person or organisation than we would be in any other role. Let's look at the difference between having one source of income, or many.

A job will bring in a source of income for as long as the company is in operation and they want you to work for them. If either of these things change, your income goes from one wage to nothing. If you like your job that's a bonus. As a self-employed professional you have many clients and many sources of income. If one of them no longer needs your help you won't lose your entire wage. You might already know this, you probably do if you're already a self-employed dog professional or have read any wise books. If you're wanting to be one, though and the fear is getting in your way, think about it!

Of course, if you have a job you love, are respected, appreciated and well paid that's great. Keep doing that. I'm talking to those who want to make the leap here - and fully acknowledge that there are many dog professionals in jobs that they love.

There are so many *rules and shoulds* involved in our very existence that we can easily believe we are getting things wrong, even when everything is perfect. Here are just some examples -

- I should take better care of my appearance

- I should be cleverer and more ambitious
- I should have more of a social life

All of these can reverberate around our mind and tell us how wrong, bad, lazy or fat we are. Yet if we give pause and ask why, there's usually no good reason for most of them.

This life on earth is yours. If you want to walk around in a muddy hoody with paw prints on the legs of your trackies all winter, do that. If you want to get your hair dyed blue do that and if you want to get lazier than you have been in ages just for the sake of it – do that.

The most important thing to do is ensure the rules you live by are your own. Not the result of nagging 'shoulds', odd glances in Tesco or feeling that your next step should be decided on what others believe is normal. Keep ethics in your heart, follow your values and decide your own path as you follow it.

Courage

Whether the changes you want to make are a promotion in your current job, packing it all in and becoming a dog walker, or building skills by going back to study after twenty years, all it takes is courage. The fun and interesting thing is that when you exercise your own courage, it's like a muscle that stretches and then strengthens, becoming fast and determined.

There's a writer called Steve Pavlina; you can find him online and I suggest you do. Steve is a font of wisdom and everything that comes out of his mouth or by his fingertips is productive and conducive to positive change. In a blog post on courage, Steve writes:

"Courageous people are still afraid, but they don't let the fear paralyze them. People who lack courage will give into fear more often than not, which actually has the long-term effect of strengthening the fear. When you avoid facing a fear and then feel relieved that you escaped it, this acts as a psychological reward that reinforces the mouse-like avoidance behaviour, making you even more likely to avoid facing the fear in the future. So, the more you avoid asking someone out on a date, the more paralyzed you'll feel about taking such actions in the future. You are literally conditioning yourself to become timid and mouse-like.

Such avoidance behaviour causes stagnation in the long run. As you get older, you reinforce your fear reactions to the point where it's hard to even imagine yourself standing up to your fears. You begin taking your fears for granted; they become real to you. You cocoon yourself into a life that insulates you from all these fears: a stable but unhappy marriage, a job that doesn't require you to take risks, an income that keeps you comfortable. Then you rationalize your behaviour: You have a family to support and can't take risks, you're too old to shift careers.

But there's something else going on behind the scenes, isn't there? That tiny voice in the back of your mind recalls that this isn't the kind of life you wanted to live. It wants more, much more.

So how do you respond to this ornery voice that won't shut up? What do you do when confronted by that gut feeling that something just isn't right in your life? What's your favourite way to silence it? Maybe drown it out by watching TV, listening to the radio, working long hours at an unfulfilling job, or consuming alcohol and caffeine and sugar"

You can read the full post at the website, all work is in the public domain, he's literally given away a huge amount of priceless content. as an act of courage of his own. He knows something you see and so do many other people. We know that it will all work out in the end. Fear is unfounded, worry is pointless premonition and life on earth is completely within our control, so if we want to do something – we just do it.

The Comfort Zone

We all have a comfort zone and as we get older, we appreciate it more. The comfort zone is a privilege and a wonderful place to be, particularly on winter nights when it's cold outside. We can imagine the comfort zone as our safe space and everyone needs one.

There is a problem though. If we stay right in the middle of our own comfort zone it gets smaller, much smaller. It can be so easy to stay inside where it's safe, not going anywhere near the edge, but nothing grows in there. If we keep to the middle of our comfort zone all the time, something strange happens. It gets ever more comfortable and the edges of it become scary. When this happens your potential is never reached and opportunities to be your best self are missed.

For example, suppose you're in a job that you hate and would like something completely different - perhaps to become a canine professional - but you won't leave your comfort zone. Even though your life has turned out nothing like you expected it to, nothing will change. You will stay unhappy in your job and never do what you really want to do, because your dream life won't come and land in your lap by itself. Yes, you will be comfortable, but you will also probably be bored, lethargic, jaded and disappointed. Particularly in the early hours or the middle of the night when you realise how unsuited to you, your life is now.

Our comfort zone can become tiny and seemingly impenetrable – it's a form of safety and control over the environment we live in. If we go towards the edge and even beyond it, we are losing that illusion of complete control that we have nurtured and where we feel safe. Yet we can venture towards the edge at any time. When we leave our comfort zone, anything can happen, and if you embrace the experience and expect the best outcome - it probably will.

If just the thought of doing something new leaves you cold, start small. Do something you haven't done before, perhaps go to the cinema on your own, or out for a coffee. Maybe you could offer dog walking services at a nearby shelter, attend a workshop or volunteer at a dog training class as an assistant. Part of leaving the comfort zone is a heightened sense of self consciousness, but that will fade as you re-enter the world of exciting new experiences.

Take a moment here and consider your life on earth, perhaps do it from the lucid dreaming pod model where everything happens in your mind, where there's no risk or real danger, just choices and the belief that everything will be just fine. What are you going to do now?

As you decide, remember this:

> *"You are braver than you believe, stronger than you seem and smarter than you think"* - Winnie The Pooh

Chapter Two
Finding Your Path

"Go confidently in the direction of your dreams! Live the life you've imagined"
- Henry David Thoreau

We are living in amazing times. Science and ancient wisdom are meeting in the world and creating unforeseen knowledge and opportunities for everyone who is willing to embrace them with courage. When I grew up there was no internet. To succeed in something like writing a book, for example, we would need to trawl around publishers and gather rejections like shards in the heart. If we wanted to discuss anything, we certainly couldn't do it with hundreds of people from our living rooms. Education was for the few who could afford it and rigid in its delivery.

Now we can learn new skills in our pyjamas, create something spectacular and take it out into the world without leaving the house. Or we can play computer games allowing people to watch and become rich by their voluntary donations. We don't have to start rich to succeed; we don't need a portfolio of certificates delivered in a rigid school education ten years ago - that mean nothing in the world today. We can just find what we love to do and do it, earning a living in the process. In fact, I would go so far as to say that it's the only thing we should do.

When you find exactly what you want to do, something amazing happens. You are led by motivation – not hindered by lack of it. When you're motivated by something specific that you love, it's not work and it rarely feels like an effort.

To find your path in the dog world, or the next step on your journey, ask yourself what you would love to do. Then consider; if there were no money and no bills to pay, would you still be doing what you're doing now?

If so, that's great. If not, why are you still doing it?

When I left school the opportunities available now to dog lovers were few. I could get a job (which is what I thought was the only possibility) in kennels, move away from home and live in at a dog care facility or work at a veterinary surgery. I ended up doing all of these and much more but didn't really enjoy any of them. I now know that I'm not suited to a job at all and believe I'll never have one again.

These day, whatever your age, your options are vast

and exciting. As a dog lover desperate for a career change, you can study and build a business based around dogs. As an established canine professional you can teach others what you already know. As a curious dog walker you can become a canine behaviour specialist via distance learning and practical application.

You can write books and self-publish them without ever getting a publisher's rejection, taking your word directly to your audience and creating a passive income from a lifetime of consistent sales. I have a friend who was long-term poorly and often housebound, yet has used her natural magic and love of dogs and created a huge Facebook page where she shares everything ethical. She's having a ball and people are approaching her with freebies and even cash, to share their goods and services.

I only ever touch, love and interact with my own dogs and never do consultations or teaching in the real world anymore. Yet through my specific skills I get to touch many dog's lives, and the life of their people, which is highly, highly motivating. My point for you is that you don't have to choose from three or four specific routes to be a dog professional. You can if they make you happy, but you don't have to. You can find a path that's different, unique even and something that no-one else has ever considered.

Let's throw some ideas around and get you thinking -

- If you love running or hiking, create a niche exercise service for energetic dogs
- Open a dog day care where enrichment is paramount
- Counsel other canine professionals on building their websites, or becoming social media experts
- Offer pet portraits or create excellent graphics for canine understanding
- Perhaps create a blog and open it up to donations
- Make a series of videos
- Coach the canine professionals
- Do good dog guardianship classes
- Organise events with excellent speakers and sell tickets
- Become a brand and sell reviews
- Create a social following for the life of your own dog and monetise it.

The options are endless for finding your exact path, the one that gets you bouncing out of bed in the mornings.

A wise thing to do is mix and match if you can. The wonder of the internet now is that we can create multiple income streams. For example, you might already be a successful and established dog walker which provides a good income, great. Yet you also have an amazing skill that would benefit others in the most spectacular ways, so why not use that skill to make a series of videos on how to create a brilliant dog walking business and offer them over the internet to people who want to make that first tenacious step into self-employment. If videos make you shrink a little, write a book. Once it's written, it's there for good and will bring a second income stream for the rest of your life, with only fundamental updates and marketing for a few minutes here and there.

Energy

For the rest of this chapter to make sense, we need to talk about energy. If you're a science mind as all the best dog people are, I ask you to suspend that for a while here. Just relax into it as I explain my model for living - life on earth - and why I choose to use it.

Humans are a biological, psychological, emotional and social animal. We all have a model for living and some serve us perfectly whilst others work against us every step of the way. The mindset dictates how we choose to live and what we believe - I'll discuss more about how we got that mindset later.

Our present mindset includes:

- How we see ourselves.
- How we see others.
- How we see the world.

We can't escape the mindset unless we learn to understand the mind, which will also be covered later. An untamed mind can take over and cause us lots of distress. The most important thing I need you to see here is that your mindset will dictate your experiences.

The model I choose as my vessel to get me around life, is energy. Just as we are biology, we are energy. The human body is made up of cells and atoms, chemistry and energy. Quantum physics is the study of the very small, the study of energy. You and I are made of energy and it radiates from us. We can also be affected by the energetic radiation of others and feel their distress if we allow it or are particularly empathetic. If you add the idea that we are simply a consciousness, moving around outside a body, it gives even more power to this model.

If you have ever seen the film Donnie Darko it explains my own model of energy and future plans perfectly. In one strange looking scene – it's a strange film to be honest. but a good one; Donnie is sitting, and a wide beam of light comes out of his chest and explores the house around him. Donnie gets up and follows it. I see that beam of light as a thought, and the act of following it without any choice, as the consequence of that thought. That's my model of living, which has been fully adopted over the last few years and serves me wonderfully.

Entrainment

Adding power to my life model is the knowledge we have on entrainment. If we consider ourselves and the world around us as energetic molecules as opposed to biological cells, we can apply entrainment to everything. Energetic molecules vibrate at a frequency and everything has its own specific frequency, including us, trees, the sea and all sounds. If we look at life and matter from this angle, you and I are the same energy vibrating in different ways. In fact, my dog and the book you're holding are also made from the same energy as you and me, we are all the same energy with different levels of vibration, we are all the same.

Entrainment was first discovered by Dutch physicist Christian Huygens in the 17th century. He noticed that a roomful of pendulum clocks would entrain from swinging in chaotic time to swinging in perfect synchronicity, without any interference. The idea behind this, is that all energy entrains to the strongest in the area.

Think about the energy in a group of people, at a

funeral, at a music festival or conference. It naturally becomes entrained and sets the mood for the event. Consider mass hysteria, protests, rallies and how we have all become such defensive drivers that we are quicker to anger when we get into the car.

In my mind model, entrainment includes my own energy and what it attracts as it goes out into the world around me. The energy starts with my thoughts, which decide its frequency, which goes out into the world and starts entraining with similar frequencies. Because I am the strongest energy there is for me, I'm likely to make the world itself entrain with my feelings. Does it sound mad? That's why it's a model and I'm not selling it to you as a fact. Anyway, if I send kind, good, positive energy out, I will attract positive and good energy back and should have a pleasant day. However, if I send out dark annoyance, I will entrain with that frequency and experience much of the same. **Basically, I'm in a dreaming pod, pure consciousness and my experiences of the world dictate how it acts towards the energetic me, who is my avatar in the game.**

I'm not saying that you must adopt this model too, or even that you should consider it a fact, it's just my choice. You don't have to find your way via a few film scenes, quantum physics and finding proof through practice. You can do it your way. I do suggest though, that you do a little research on energy and accept that your life will always go where your mind goes first, as this can be accepted by even the most scientific of minds.

The Beauty of Ideas

Ideas are amazing! J.K. Rowling had an idea and made it into solid form for years, gathering rejections along the way. Yet she maintained it and worked on it, enhancing millions of lives for the better. Everything that we do, or that others have done began as an idea.

Imagine that ideas float around in the air between us. They are little clouds of magic that occasionally land on your or me, giving us a choice. We can grab the idea and run with it, or we can ignore it or leave it for so long that it moves on – dying in our minds.

The book you're reading right now was an idea that landed on me recently. It started as a little thought that twinkled. It landed on my shoulder and said, "why not write a book for the people this time" so I started writing there and then, and here it is.

Two years ago, I was writing for an amazing lady who founded an amazing, affordable and ethical online learning portal, and my husband was working as a shop manager. After another bad day at work for him, an idea landed on me and I blurted it out there and then. "Why don't you leave your job and we can create dog courses together?" Thankfully after thought and batting away the fear, he liked that idea and Canine Principles was born. It was a success from the outset and has changed our lives tremendously, helping people and dogs along the way.

What do you do when a magic idea visits you? How many have you ignored, only to see someone else putting them into form a few months later? Do you have an idea right now that's fizzing on your shoulder, whispering in your ear and waiting for you to do something with it? Are you going to act? If not, why not?

Money

Money does strange things to people for no real reason at all. Just like there are with life on earth, there are social rules associated with money and ideas about it. We hear sayings like "money is power" or "money is the root of all evil" and if heard often enough we believe them. So we shy away from admitting that we want a lot of money because we believe it makes us greedy, selfish or inherently bad. Here's the fact on that; money doesn't make us anything. It is completely neutral.

If someone is going to act badly towards someone else based on being motivated by money, they are likely to act badly when motivated by anything at all. If someone is good and motivated by helping people, they are going to do that whether they have money or not.

Assess how you view money and ask yourself whether you associate it with evil, scarcity, power or inequality. Do you complain about money and about those who have too much, do you get worked up about paying your taxes? Or do you like money but it slips through your fingers? Perhaps you are putting off a life change, purely based on fear of not having enough money afterwards?

If you have already started thinking about your life model, I urge you to add your thoughts and feelings about money into your exploration, because if your mind always goes to scarcity, so will your life. Be wise with money, treat it with respect, don't be frivolous or wasteful but don't be uptight and worried either. Perhaps make a rule to never complain about money again, to never say that you can't afford something, because those are powerful words.

I love money, well not quite – I love money energy. In my own mind model, I see cash floating around like ideas. Money is limitless because it's not real – we can give it away and if we believe it to be so, it will come back. We can take risks with it, because it's everywhere and nowhere, like the gold coins in Mario world. It might seem a little odd, particularly if you live with scarcity, but stick with me here. Living in scarcity is often accompanied by a desire to inherit or win some big money that will change our life. Here's the fact; you don't need to win, you can change your life anyway.

If you follow your true path, embrace your own unique, precious skill set, follow good ideas with inspired action and handle money wisely, your income will rise along the way. And you know what, it will become normal to have more than you need. So you will start giving it away, which in my experience is the very best bit!

Chapter Three
Think Carefully

"Very little is needed to make a happy life; it is all within yourself, in your way of thinking" - Marcus Aurelius

If you're particularly science focussed you will be pleased to know this chapter moves back onto solid ground and away from flying money and ideas with wings. The mind is a huge topic and one that every single person will benefit from understanding better.

Within everyone of there are a number of things that we must get right to be peaceful and truly happy. When we work with dogs this is essential, we must *'mind our minds'*. Knowledge give you power over mind chatter which has the power to change how you feel, act and react.

"So, the single most vital step on your journey toward enlightenment is this: learn to de-identify from your mind."
- Eckhart Tolle

Eckhart Tolle is a German teacher who wrote a book called The Power of Now. He's wonderful and his focus is always on living right in the moment, mindfulness and literally, the acceptance that the moment we are in is all there is. It's a mind model but it's also the truth – because no-one can prove otherwise as despite our technology, we haven't learned to time travel yet.

The human mind is fascinating, yet can be our friend or foe. To understand it properly we must first consider the grey matter. The brain is programmed to avoid danger and seek safety. We have evolved this way and it's the reason we are here, because if our ancestors didn't expect a dangerous tiger from every rock they encountered, they became lunch. There were probably happy go lucky cavemen who waltzed through life without a care in the world; they were probably eaten. The careful survived and eventually their genes became ours.

So when your mind screams "watch out, this isn't safe enough", ask yourself, is it really a tiger or is it just your perception of a harmless rock?

In addition to what the psychologists call our negative bias, we also have a brain and body that are susceptible to stress. If you have studied the stress reaction in dogs, then you already understand this. Stress shouldn't be underestimated - it can kill people.

A wise man said to me recently, on the topic of reading glasses, that he doesn't believe our bodies have quite caught up with our lifestyles. His theory on the matter was that the ability to read small words on smaller screens is, according to our bodies, irrelevant to our overall survival at this point in time. In the same way, we could assume this of general stress.

Stress originates in the brain and the nervous system. It's useful in circumstances where an energetic burst for survival is helpful. The brain produces cortisol and the muscles join its quest for strength by filling with precious adrenaline. When we get stressed by something, we are experiencing a biological and psychological fight or flight reaction, a super strength for survival. I remember standing on the start line of my first ever half marathon, hearing the pistol and feeling adrenaline rush into my legs. It was an odd feeling, that simple biological preparation produced by my mind for the task my body was facing and completely outside my control.

Most of us spend up to eighty years or more experiencing no real physical danger from outside ourselves. We may perceive it from within; we could perhaps suffer a real near miss such as a close call accident, yet the reason for true fight or flight is rare. So why are we all so easily stressed? I think it's because we have nowhere to put the evolved reaction that has kept us safe for thousands of years, which is a topic we shall return to later.

Humans are actually time travellers and we do it all the time, a habit that does us no good at all. I often wonder whether dogs are time travellers too; they may be but probably don't ruminate as we do. Our own time travelling can bring us joy or dread, fear or laughter.

We have the ability to go with our mind anywhere we see. Not from a pod in a life model but from your seat, bed or desk where you are right now. The mind is friend and foe. I best heard it described as the chimp in the iconic mind management book The Chimp Paradox. Your mind isn't you, nor is it separate from you, but it does have a significant effect on how you feel. Your mind is your consciousness and your gremlin, it's the chatter and the whisper. Your mind can make or break you depending on how it uses your thoughts and whether you make friends with it or not.

We are all different and I can't possibly experience what happens in your head, just as you can't experience what happens in mine. However, we do know that a lot of us have the same issues with those reckless, random and unkind thoughts. We are also aware that they are likely to never stop. If you're blessed with a busy mind that can be a blessing or a curse.

Attachment

When we are born, the first experiences that we have set the brain on its growth path. It's thought that from the moment we are born, whether we are left to cry out or comforted makes a difference on how well we can trust later on. John Bowlby (1907 - 1990) was a psychoanalyst who presented a theory called The Attachment Theory. Primarily related to maternal care Bowlby believed that unless we received positive response to our solicitation of affection and contact from our primary attachment figure – note, not just food – right up until we are two years old, we will suffer later on. The behaviours that Bowlby theorised we were at risk of developing without positive attachment in those crucial first two years included:

- Affectionless psychopathy, a lack of empathy and the inability to show true affection to others.
- Delinquency, antisocial acts and behaviour.
- Depression, isolation and bad thoughts including rumination.
- Increased aggression or tendency to anger.
- Reduced intelligence and the inability to fulfil true potential.

Remember though, this is only a theory. Although it has been recreated a number of times on smaller animals and shown to have some significance, we can make any theory fit ourselves if we want to, and sometimes that's not a bit helpful.

There are many other theories that the psychoanalyst community has offered us over the years. Freud is one of the most famous ones and whilst his ideas on everything being related to sex are a little out there, he did bring us the foundations that were to become positive change. Freud bought us talking therapy at its most basic form, an approach that was to become Cognitive Behaviour Therapy and has become very helpful indeed.

The reason I'm telling you this is to give you some understanding on how long the mind has been studied and how early learning can affect the mind's behaviour. This may give you a little more understanding of how your own thoughts got to where they are now.

Just as we already explored, the mind has a mindset which determines the nature of our thoughts.

Let's take a closer look at that now:

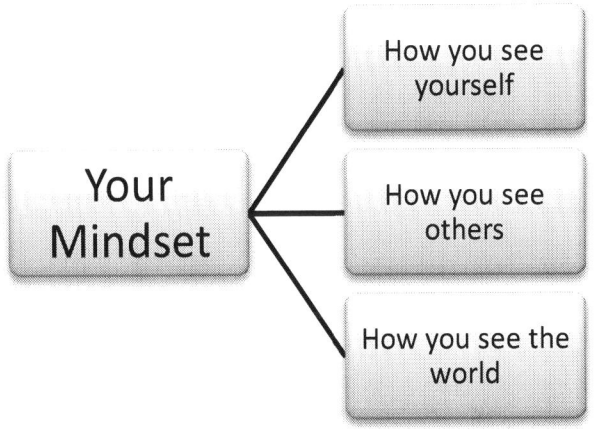

For this exercise, try assuming that there are two of you in your head. One is the true you and the other is your mind. Give him a name if you must, I'll call him the wild mind – and 'him' for convenience.

How do you see yourself? More importantly though, does the way that you see yourself serve you? Do you see yourself through a true, real lens, or is your idea about yourself at the mercy of a wild mind? Symptoms that a wild mind may be dictating the image you have of yourself include lack of self-belief, low self-esteem and being critical of yourself.

How do you see others? Are they selfish, awkward zombies or individuals that you just haven't made friends with yet? Do you expect the best from strangers or the worst?

Here's an example of experiencing others – from our world. A common thing that dog people learn about other people on walks, is that they have little empathy towards dogs beyond their own. When we are out walking with our scared little dogs, people let their dogs run up without control. It's happened many times and now we expect it. So in this instance, we see others as thoughtless, mindless beasts. It's a sweeping generalisation based on frustration and fear, and it's reinforced regularly. So it's easy to think that this is how other people are when really, they are not. Many walk by with their dogs under close control. They see us and take a different path or recall their dogs perfectly. Yet we expect all of them to be thoughtless. This affects how we feel about other dog walkers in general and makes our walks tense when we see someone else. This type of expectation is born from experience. Years ago when I had a bomb proof dog, I didn't mind friendly loose dogs and neither did she, so walks were much more relaxing. Now though, we would take a shuttle to the moon for a daily hike if we could.

Have a think about how you see others, both those close to you and strangers. Do you expect your partner to run away with an interesting stranger one day? Perhaps you think all doctor's receptionists guard the surgery like their life depends on it. Maybe you live an adult version of what we were taught as five-year-old kids "stranger danger" or maybe as you have got older you simply don't like anyone anyway. I promise you that whatever you expect from others – they will deliver it on the most basic level, because your expectation will dictate your conduct in the interaction, and your conduct will dictate theirs.

How do you see the world? Is it a beautiful place to be filled with wonder and miracles, such as the huge oak which grows from a tiny acorn, or is it a dangerous place that you try to hide from – in your own little corner of it?

I suggest you take some time and brainstorm answers to these two questions. Whether you write your answers on a bit of paper, a file on your pc or dictate them into your phone, really doesn't matter. The important bit is that you put them outside of yourself so that you can view and assess them properly.

When you have your answers, ask yourself if you really think these things, from your true mind or is your wild mind dictating every experience in your life? The wild mind is a simple beast. He wants to keep you safe, has a huge ego and is extremely defensive – if your answers reflect these (wonderfully low) quality traits, it's likely your wild mind is running the show. He's the one who gets angry at other drivers, that huffs and puffs in shops and he has the worst expectations of other dog walkers – even when they are half a mile away and already going in the other direction.

Having established how much power that wild mind has over your life, let's work on your relationship with him.

It's important to remember that we are working on a series of models throughout this book, so often my advice and descriptions are not literal, they are models for understanding that we can apply, for positive understanding and change.

Mindfulness

Mindfulness is the choice to be fully present in your mind, in a series of moments. It's an ancient skill that takes practice, particularly important if you live with a wild mind and he runs the show a lot of the time.

The opposite of mindfulness is mindlessness. A lot of people live mindlessly and it's the basis of tension in crowds and supermarkets. When mindless, we wander around thinking of something else, not engaged at all with the current task, getting in the way of others and losing all idea that there's not only us in the world.

On the subject of mindlessness in our society, we have a running joke in our house, my husband's sod's law. If he goes to a huge shop with one other person in it, they will be stood directly in front of the only item he is there to purchase. If he's on a walk and politely waits for someone to pass through a gate, they will take off their backpacks and lean up the gate for a rest, blocking his way, I have seen it with my own eyes and it's completely true. Interestingly, the world around him is filling his expectations perfectly and he's either sending that type of energy into the world or he's only noticing the sod's law events, depending on which model we view his experience from. Either way his expectations have indeed become his reality in the funniest and most frustrating way.

Mindlessness is not being fully present in the mind at any moment. Many of us are barely present in our lives at all, which is such a waste of the opportunity to appreciate the wonders of life on earth. Mindlessness also renders us totally vulnerable to the nagging, whispering voice of the wild mind.

We are living in exciting times. Times where ancient practices join modern medicine to raise the consciousness and wellness of our species. One of these ancient practices is mindfulness, which is a simple practice that takes learning but will change your experiences of life on earth.

Proven time and again to help and alleviate depression, anxiety and many other conditions based in the wild mind, mindfulness is an amazing and life-changing practice. Mindfulness based CBT is replacing just CBT in many healthcare environments. We now see everything from mindful colouring books to meditation classes available on prescription, because this stuff really works.

Achieving mindfulness is like everything else we do for the first time, it takes practice and becomes easier the more we do it. Practiced mindfulness is called meditation, which simply means a specific bit of time we can put aside to get fully inside our minds. When we are fully inside our minds, we can recognise that wild mind voice of destructive thinking patterns. Whilst we can't shut him up for good, we can learn to stop his whisperings affecting how we feel, which is where his real power is.

To make this a little clearer, let's take a look at how the wild mind can change our experiences:

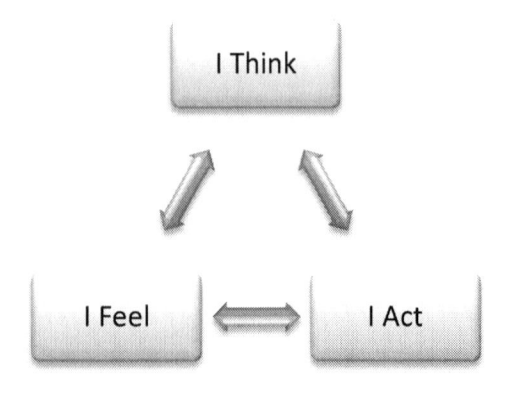

```
        I Think
       ↙      ↘
   I Feel ⇔ I Act
```

To explain the above classic CBT model further, think about presumptions. To presume that a person feels a certain way means that we don't give them a chance to tell us or show us how they feel, we respond based on how we think they feel. So immediately we are acting under a misapprehension.

If you were to see someone you knew and liked for the first time in a long time and they walked past you without acknowledgement, you are left with a choice. You can either assume that their lack of acknowledgement is caused by their busy mind or presume that you have somehow upset them. If you choose the latter – which is usually a symptom of the wild mind and his defensive view, you will indeed join him in his defensiveness. You might feel confused then angry at their (perceived) ignorance and next time you bump into them you might be short and cross with them, even when they say hello. You are now presenting a behaviour that changes their opinion of you, based on a misconception of them resulting in an all-round bad experience, that was ignited by one wild thought that took hold in your mind.

If you had chosen the former option which is harmless to you, because their absence of mind really has nothing to do with you, your experience would be quite different. You might stop them and say hi, ask if they are ok and have a quick catch-up chat which makes you feel good. Your wild mind may be huffing and puffing - with his arms crossed - but that doesn't matter.

Both of these options have something important in common. Your thoughts will affect the way you feel and as soon as you feel differently you will act differently. This change in behaviour will affect the world around you and the people in it, it will affect your experience of life on earth. The most interesting thing is the whole encounter and consequence from it, begins as one thought, in one moment.

This brings us directly back to mindfulness. When we practice being mindful, we just have to give pause and clarify the moment. It's an amazing tool to bring into your life and there are many courses on it, ranging from free to hundreds of pounds for the study of it.

The most helpful practice that I have found within the mindfulness concept is a small yet wonderfully effective set of principles by Scottish teacher Sydney Banks.

The Three Principles

I believe The Three Principles by Sydney Banks to be the simplest mind management tool that we have access to today. I strongly suggest that you explore it further. Sydney set out three principles for living that are still being taught and presented all over the world. I learned the basis through the work of Michael Neill who has some accessible books available on the topic.

Again, this is a model I use regularly when thoughts get chaotic and those nasty little whisperings pop into my mind from nowhere. You may need to take some time to mull these principles over as they really do seem too simple to understand. Keep at it though, because if you do they will flash into your mind as a eureka moment and change your life. Once understood, you will have constant access to this priceless tool as presented below:

The Mind

The mind is presented as the universal mind. The power and energy of all endlessness and possibility. The wonder of a mind where we can send thoughts into the world and our life on earth will follow them without fail. The mind is powerful, energetic, intelligent and committed to a oneness with all things, it has the power to create your world from inside, endlessly. When you are fully at one with your own universal mind and its power, you cannot help but meet your dreams with nothing but unflinching belief that they are already yours.

Consciousness

Consciousness or awareness is the knowledge of the power of your mind and the nature of your thoughts. To be conscious is your key to using the most magical aspects of your true mind by knowing that they exist and being able to separate mind from thought.

Thought

Thought is described by Sydney Banks as the rudder that will guide you through life. By acknowledging and understanding that thoughts are not set in reality, but can dictate our reality, we are empowered to choose the thoughts that serve us and wait for the ones that don't, to naturally pass. Which interestingly is also the basis of mindfulness.

The most important thing about this particular model is that no matter whether you practice it or not, it's always happening. Whether your thoughts affect your life on earth via the practical example given above, or whether they affect you because you believe they are your future enough to make your ideas happen, Syd's Principles are always happening. Study, explore and investigate this enough and one day it will flood into your mind like a light has been switched on. It will be a moment when everything suddenly becomes easier to understand and apply to your life.

It's really interesting when Syd's principles sink in. Suddenly you see the world, other people and nature through a lens of total clarity when a wild thought whispers into your mind, threatening the foundation of your wellbeing. A thought that would usually trigger guilt, sadness or hopelessness; you can now simply say "this too shall pass". We can't stop our thoughts and we can't resist them with strength or an inner battle, but we can recognise what they are and still maintain peace of mind whilst they become self-neutralised in the background. This is a wonderful skill that prevents the wild mind changing how we feel and maintains a peaceful and enlightened experience of our life on earth.

When this model is accepted and embraced, we are able to hold a new respect and understanding of others too. The acceptance that we are all one universal mind triggers a new empathy for others. Rather than seeing them as a threat, we realise that they have their own reasons for what they do. This is a powerful realisation indeed.

The Magic Moment

Imagine that this moment is your entire life, how do you feel? Are you thinking of the next one or the last one? I say imagine because this acceptance may be completely new to you, although it's the simplest and most delicious thing to know.

The key to mindfulness is not imagining that this moment is all there is - but accepting it.

If a giant pink elephant approached you right now and granted you ten final moments before you moved onto the next step of your universal journey, telling you that one moment will move directly into another and they are so precious because they are limited to ten, how many of them would you spend worrying about tomorrow or next week? How many would you spend regretting and feeling guilty about something that happened thirty years ago. How many would you delve directly into and enjoy?

Everyone's answer to this question will be different.

Some of us are habitual worriers and can project much doom and gloom into the future. I have thoughts about leaving my dogs at home alone, which doesn't happen very often. When we do leave them alone my wild mind is throwing "what if's" at me all the time we are away.

Here's another interesting story, I live with a weird dread that the car boot will open whilst we are driving with the dogs in the back. Over the last few weeks it's become stronger and I have checked it religiously, even after we have started the trip, to my husband's dismay. A few days ago, the car boot started opening on its own with an electrical fault that has now been fixed, Did I cause the fault? Who knows, but I urge you to mind your thoughts carefully just in case.

Others have things in the past or people in their lives now who are associated with guilt. It's more common than you may think. For example, we might have a moment of pure joy and naturally default to being guilty for feeling happy. So even the nicest experiences take us through a process that ends up with bleak despair. Even if we don't consciously know why we feel a sudden abject misery at the moment we feel elation, this association could be sitting quietly, waiting to pounce – as soon as we feel happy enough.

A common example of this - for us dog people - could be something like getting dressed up for the first time in months, going somewhere nice and really enjoying ourselves, until a flash of guilt that the dogs are home alone triggers an instant mood drop. The dog is fine, nothing has changed in that moment, other than how we feel. Or you may remember a dog in your past like I did once. I saw a German Shepherd in town the other day and the sight of him transported me back to a dog I lost in the army, 25 years ago. I instantly experienced desperate sadness and a perfect example of why time travel is not good for us.

There is a biology behind our warped thinking though and knowing the biology is a fundamental step towards exercising consciousness and self-empowerment. If you have read any of my work on dog behaviour, this will be familiar to you.

Everything we do becomes an established route through our brain, a neural pathway. The more we take that route, the easier it is to take. This applies to every choice, every thought pattern and experience we have. Imagine it like an ancient overgrown garden. The gardens are so overgrown that you can't find a route through them, so you have to make one. The biological equivalent to this is your first experience or choice in a brand-new situation.

You make a choice to go in a specific direction so fight your way through the weeds and grass to get to where you want to be. You have created a rough pathway, which is easier to take next time.

The pathways you practice most become your habits. They are so easy to take after choosing them a few times that you don't even consider that there might be an easier way, or one that serves you better.

Let's look at a scenario where this can get out of control. A mother and adult child have a rocky relationship. The child has gone into the world and achieved many things. The mother has stayed where she grew up and become dissatisfied and unhappy, voicing her misery at every opportunity. The child from the age of early teens has enjoyed their life but guilt has plagued them along the way. They may have been enjoying something and then remembered their mother sitting sad at home and consciously experienced guilt. Fast forward thirty years and the adult child has accepted that their mother's life is not their responsibility, in all but the most subconscious way. Now though, if they feel any happiness at all, that neural pathway that has been used for all of their adult life bypasses the guilt altogether. Every single time they feel happy, the younger adult feels extremely sad too.

Unless we make a conscious effort to understand the habit and biology associated with this type of default thinking it can ruin our lives. There is excellent news though, neuroplasticity never ends.

Changing Your Brain

Neuroplasticity describes the brains ability to change, grow and respond to stimulation. It includes the ability to change neural pathways and form new ones, in response to learning something new. Imagine the brain like plasticine, it can be shaped, moulded and changed.

Early in our lives, neuroplasticity is vast, and changes

are happening at an alarming rate. We used to believe that it stopped in adulthood, but it doesn't. New brain matter and neuro-pathways can be created all the time if we get the stimulation right. So, we can go to university at the age of fifty and learn enough to get an excellent degree. We can learn to drive at the age of sixty and we can undo those nasty little neutral pathways that make us unhappy, at any time in our lives.

The beauty of this biology is that we can actually teach ourselves to return to the moment we are in at any time, and leave the sadness, guilt or worry in another moment. So, rather than walking a group of dogs and feeling bad about something that happened last week we can walk the dogs and feel good about the experience we are having, because it's literally all there is.

There's something wonderful about assessing your own neural pathways too. If a crippling sadness hits you about something you did years ago, telling yourself that it's a neural pathway and not actually happening now, is empowerment. It's just biology.

If you have ever seen the short film 'Tough Love a Meditation on Dominance and Dogs', you may relate to the wonderful (and sadly late) Sophia Yin's words at the opening of the film. Sophia was a veterinarian and clinical dog behaviourist who revolutionised understanding of dog behaviour. She tells us in the film that her first dog was trained by old-fashioned methods, under the guidance of bad trainers and because she thought their methods were fact, she did everything they asked. In a poignant confession that reduced her to tears even years later, she felt that the methods had spoiled her dog's potential for the rest of his life. Sophia committed suicide a few years ago and was a terrible loss to the positive dog world.

Maybe you lived and taught dogs in the times when punishment was considered normal? When the alpha wolf theory was considered truth (shudder) and you followed the rules, like Sophia did, you too may have deep regrets. I was an army dog trainer and whilst I was never extreme to dogs, back then I thought checking was normal and practiced it alongside everyone else, something of which I'm deeply ashamed. If you have hidden shame about earlier methods, don't let it haunt you now. It's gone and the only way it can make you suffer is if you allow it into this moment right now. It's just biology and remembrance of your thoughts, this too shall pass.

Here's something interesting, meditation and mindfulness is proven to increase neuroplasticity. So, by learning to be mindful and practicing it through meditation, you can change your physical brain. Over the last few years studies on mindfulness learned through meditation have shown amazing results, which include:

- Increased ability to stop the mind wandering beyond the moment we are in, resulting in more power over regrets, worries and fearful projections of the future.
- Meditation has been shown to improve the ability to focus and learn, in as little as two weeks practice.
- The Amygdala – the brain's stress area – has been shown to reduce in size and cellular production with practiced meditation, leading to stress reduction.
- The hippocampus is shown to be increased in thickness by a few weeks of regular meditation, this leads to more control over emotions.
- The practice has shown great potential to reduce anxiety and social anxiety in a few different studies, by quietening the 'me-centric' area of the brain. This is the area that we so far have called the wild mind, associated with extreme emotional reaction and defensiveness to ensure survival.

Meditation is the act of unplugging from the world and just focussing on the moment as a form of practiced mindfulness. It can slow your heart rate, brainwaves, and thoughts to the point that they seem to be gone for a while and certainly lose all power over how you feel. A simple meditation practice can be carried out by sitting or lying somewhere quiet – with a straight spine - and counting your breaths to 100. If your mind wanders just come back to your breath and continue to count, allowing the chatter to continue in the background.

Chapter Four
Life with a Wild Mind

"Forget past mistakes. Forget failures. Forget about everything except what you're going to do now - and do it."
- William Durant

You may have read the last chapter and finished it thinking, "a bit of meditation won't help with my huge amount of issues". You might even have suffered with diagnosed mental illness for a long time. Or perhaps you are physically unwell and believe you have no control over that? It's for that reason I decided to delve deeper into mental wellness, how it's linked with physical wellness and how we can help ourselves, no matter how extreme our problems are.

There are a few things that can detract from achieving true mental wellness and wellbeing. Conditions such as depression, anxiety and long-term stress can be debilitating and if they show up as symptoms in the mind, they will almost certainly also appear in the body.

I'm not going to give a list of instructions here, or some pushy advice that tells you to exercise or eat raw vegan food and all your symptoms will go away. There's enough of that in the world, isn't there? What I'm going to do is tell you what has been found out about mental wellness in the last few years and let you make up your own mind.

Depression

Depression is hard to live with. There are a number of theories on why it occurs and there is still a stigma attached to the presence of depression. People often tell each other to buck-up and stop wallowing, with the idea that it's imaginary and the sufferer can just stop. Another idea is that depression may well be real but by getting out of bed, self-grooming and changing what we eat and do in the daytime, we can beat it. The big problem with that is that we simply don't feel like it. When depression strikes, it's guilt, despair, lethargy and overwhelm, so to be hit with a bunch of rules and tasks is completely counter-productive when even the smallest job is too big to tackle.

I have Seasonal Depression which was diagnosed about ten years ago. I remember going to the GP with another bout of crippling sadness and striking lucky for the first time, because he was a mental health professional and recognised the symptoms immediately. Seasonal depression is like any other type, it's a reduction of serotonin production in the brain. This particular one is due to lack of light entering the inner eye. For me, knowledge was power and now I don't only live with it, I embrace it. Some days I work in my pyjamas all day long and other days I don't work at all. I have a lightbox which is sitting on my desk beaming at me right now and I take medication through the winter too. I don't eat raw vegan food for every meal (although I am vegan) I don't do the hour's exercise a day that I should and whilst I know the classic wellness rules would help, and probably reduce the need for medication - I'm human and doing what works for me without a scrap of guilt. Which is exactly my point to you.

It can be easy to read a new book or encounter someone's experience and state to anyone that will listen "right, I'm going to make all these life changes and I will no longer suffer with this" We might fill the cupboards with fresh food and fruit, we could buy a treadmill and make a promise to use it every day. We tend to go extreme with things like this and then after a short time everything is back to normal and we feel like a failure. So, I say to you, hand on heart, do the things that make you feel good and don't worry too much about the rest.

If you stay in bed until midday on a day off, enjoy

every moment and don't feel guilty about it. If you eat the whole six portion cake in one afternoon, great, enjoy it. We often treat ourselves to something frivolous or well over-indulgent, sometimes for days or weeks, all the time feeling fraught with tension because we believe we shouldn't be making that choice. You know what though? It really doesn't matter. Eating the cake with a constant nagging regret, even as it goes into your mouth, is depriving yourself of the pleasure it brings - and I bet you are so distracted by those grim, nonsense thoughts that you can barely taste the cake anyway.

I urge you to do exactly what you want to do in every area of your life, and embrace the colourful, random, relaxing, indulgent and lazy experiences along the way. However – and this is an important point – do it from a point of knowledge and informed accurate awareness.

There has been an overhaul of how depression is treated in the last few years. In the past, counselling and therapy would unpack past experiences, over and over again. We believed that talking over bad experiences would result in lessening their power over us. Now we know that re-visiting bad experiences takes us back along the neural pathway, which is literally reliving them over and over again, resulting in a perpetuation of the cycle of depressive thinking.

Practicing depression by consistently reliving bad experiences is called rumination. We can ruminate all on our own and many of us do, we certainly don't need a therapist for it. Thankfully though, most therapy and treatment for depression has moved away from rumination and asks the question, "what are you going to do now?".

Mindfulness and meditation is increasingly part of depression treatment plans. Exercise is also prescribed a lot for people suffering with depression. In the UK, we can literally now be prescribed a membership of a private gym or a weight loss club, by our local GP.

Depression is lack of serotonin production in the brain. Serotonin is a neurotransmitter linked to positive feelings and resilience. Why it stops being produced hasn't been agreed on yet but it's likely to be a number of reasons and each one will depend on the individual sufferer's reason for becoming depressed. For example, reactive depression may be experienced due to grief after loss of a loved one. Clinical depression may be caused by a biological issue in the brain structure or seasonal depression means that there's not enough light getting to the brain. There may be more than one reason that serotonin is not sufficient enough to lift mood.

The reason that many professionals are looking toward diet and lifestyle as a treatment for depression is their ability to raise serotonin production in the brain. Medication will also prevent serotonin from being re-absorbed into the brain before it's done its important job.

Mental health medication in my opinion has revolutionised healthcare; before it was discovered, people with depression were still being forced into foreboding Victorian asylums and treatments such as electric shock therapy to the temples. Long, lukewarm baths that lasted for days were considered treatment, whilst being continually sedated or even lobotomised where part of the frontal cortex was destroyed by pushing a needle in through the eye. Shortly after pharmaceutical breakthroughs occurred, many of the asylums were closed down. It's quite unthinkable now isn't it, that we may once have been lobotomised for being depressed?

Stress

We can categorise stress into three areas, one more than dogs because as far as we know, dogs are not fortune tellers or big on time travel, whilst we are excellent at both.

Short term stress is useful because it brings extra strength when we need it. For example, when we have to think clearly to achieve something. Short term stress is physical and mental. It's based in the mind and body and is the result of evolution that gave us a boost to survive in the presence of a threat. If you have experienced this type of stress you will know that you felt clear minded and strong for a short while, then it either overwhelmed you or died down. When short term stress goes beyond the point of excellent performance, usually when the situation goes too far outside of our control, overwhelm kicks in and we lose the useful peak of awareness.

Long term stress is damaging because it's repeated episodes of short term stress that often become long term overwhelm. The body stops coping with the influx of stress chemicals. Long term stress is extremely serious and can result in heart disease, stroke and many other illnesses. If we live a life that is stressful and don't ever have the opportunity to recover, we can develop long term stress and experience some of the following points:

- A constant onslaught of bad thoughts.
- A jaded view towards things you may have once enjoyed.
- Fear and anxiety.
- Feeling aggressive.
- Feeling constantly overwhelmed.
- Feeling highly emotional.
- Irritation.

- Lack of interest in life.
- Loneliness.
- Pessimism.
- Self-medicating through drugs and alcohol.
- The development of depression.

There are many physical symptoms of stress too. We often don't consider physical changes to be part of poor mental health, particularly if we don't have much experience of it. However, it makes sense that a reaction grown from the nervous system to keep us safe, will change the body in many ways too.

Signs from the body that long term stress is present, may include:

- Chest pains.
- Digestive problems.
- Dizziness.
- Fainting.
- Feeling tired all the time.
- Headaches.
- High blood pressure.
- Insomnia.
- Nausea.
- Panic attacks.
- Sore eyes and/or blurred eyesight.
- Teeth grinding or jaw tension.

- Tension in the body, particularly the muscles.

Any of the above symptoms may indicate that your stress system is out of sync and you need to address it. If you suffer with many of the symptoms, you need to seek medical help whilst also making long-term changes towards developing resilience in your life.

The third type of stress, which is the one that only humans suffer with – as far as we know – is indicative of the wild mind taking over your true self. The mind is powerful and can easily convince the body of danger where there is none. By ruminating through fear, fortune telling a bad outcome or reliving stressful times, the mind will dictate a physical reaction in the body. It only needs to convince the body that the stressful experience is happening in this moment, something which its very good at.

There are many examples of the mind changing the body. Placebo drug trials and even operations, where the mind has been convinced of healing have shown that if the mind believes the body will follow. Trials that wouldn't be accepted in today's society such as feigned heart or knee surgery, resulted in spontaneous healing despite the surgery have never taken place. Athletes that are walked through performance in their mind, whilst lying completely still show the same muscles firing as if they were physically competing.

In the same way, if we spend a lot of time in thought patterns that are associated with or trigger stress, the body will experience the same stress reaction for one single event over and over again. When we live with stress in this way it changes how we act and feel, so it changes our environment which results in people acting differently towards us, creating more stress.

Most of us have encountered someone who is difficult to be around because there is always a drama or problem. They tend to talk a lot and overreact to things. These people tend to always have a problem with the behaviour or simply the presence of someone specific, but their target person changes regularly.

The energetic presence of someone like this is exhausting. They can also be harmful to be around if you have low self-esteem because all of their own behaviour is projected in blame towards others. In reality though, this person is suffering constantly and may even be completely addicted to their own stress reaction, because in their perception of it, it keeps them safe. In essence, their behaviour is like that of a dog that reacts towards stressors with a defensiveness because it believes that keeps them safe too. Unfortunately, without looking inwards and taking responsibility for their feelings and actions nothing will change for this type of stress sufferer. Their relationships will suffer, and their physical health will be a problem for the entirety of their lives, which is very sad indeed. We will talk more about how to manage being around others later.

We don't have to direct our attention towards others though, to relive the same stressful experience over and over again. We can do it with anything at all. Post Traumatic Stress Disorder is an example of an extreme stress that becomes burned into our experience and repeats as if on a loop. I believe that when we lose a dog to age, accident or illness, we go through a PTSD response where we relive the situation of loss over and over as part of the healing process. But if it doesn't heal as part of natural grief, the experience will loop forever unless it's dealt with.

Examples of life-changing PTSD are experiences in war, highly traumatic experiences and being part of a natural or man-made disaster. The experience in long-term PTSD is linked to a newly formed neural pathway in the brain, that is travelled when triggered over and over again. It leads to small triggers that cause highly distressing re-enactments of the original stress experience, in the body and mind, despite the sufferer being completely safe with no threats in the moment at all.

Mindfulness is increasingly used as part of treatment for stress reduction. In fact, many of the modern therapy types have incorporated mindfulness into treatment plans, acknowledging that every experience begins first in the mind and that if we understand thoughts first we become much more empowered to understand the rest.

Anxiety

Anxiety is sometimes called Generalised Anxiety Disorder and approximately 5% of people in the United Kingdom suffer with it. It is thought that a sufferer whose parents or grandparents suffered with GAD are five times more likely to suffer too. Unlike depression which tends to slow the thinking, in some ways protecting us from the wild mind, anxiety is characterised by fast and overwhelming thought patterns that provide no respite. Whilst it can be treated with medication and talking therapies, anxiety has no one known defined cause.

It's considered that the following may be contributors to the condition:

- A history of trauma or abuse.
- Addiction, prior or present.
- Being bullied in the past or present.
- Brain over-activity specifically in emotional and behavioural areas.
- Genetic influence.

- Long-term pain.
- Unbalanced brain chemicals that affect and maintain mood, including serotonin and noradrenaline.

Anxiety is currently treated with a bespoke treatment plan which can be inclusive of medication, talking therapies, exercise, nutritional therapy and growth of resilience.

Compassion Fatigue

The reason we have covered the above conditions is because of the high risk in our industry of compassion fatigue, which could easily become one or more of the above mental health conditions. Even if you have never suffered, mental health awareness is paramount to understanding yourself and others.

Compassion fatigue awareness is especially relevant to people working in rescue and highly emotional positions, veterinary nurses and veterinarians are susceptible to the condition too.

Compassion fatigue is experienced when we are exposed to upsetting situations and circumstances time and again, to the point where upset becomes so natural that it seems to be our normal state. Where we would normally feel pretty good, we may be jaded instead. The basis of compassion fatigue is an empathy type known as personal distress.

Empathy is the ability to take an interest in and understand the situation from the viewpoint of someone else, usually someone who is suffering, human or animal. It's split into two types:

- Cognitive empathy is the act of empathising with someone through your mind and thoughts. This takes the viewpoint of understanding without causing too much pain for the person experiencing it. This type of empathy is generally an objective experience.
- Emotional empathy is where we literally feel the suffering of the individual sufferer. This is a much more intensive experience, leading to general sadness and compassion fatigue. We can see someone suffering and experience their personal distress through our own emotional response.

People that are attracted to caring roles, such as dog care, veterinary nursing or even care of vulnerable people seem to be particularly susceptible to personal distress when experiencing empathy. We often also 'feel' the energy of someone that's suffering, so can't really explain why we suddenly feel sad. If that sadness is repeated daily though, as it is when we work with scared or abused dogs, or people that are suffering because their dogs are ill or similar experiences, we get fatigued.

Thankfully, compassion fatigue is recognised much more that it once was. It's vitally important if you're in a care-giving team, to look for signs of it in yourself or others. If you work alone, you are also at risk because you lack the social benefits of shared experiences. It's vital to practice awareness and self-awareness through emotional intelligence which we will discuss a little later.

Compassion Fatigue Symptoms

There are many symptoms that indicate compassion fatigue might be present or developing. It can go one of two ways when it starts and either way should be addressed quickly by self-care and professional help if possible. The following symptoms indicate compassion fatigue:

- A feeling of burden when encountering others who are suffering.
- A sense of blame towards someone that is suffering.
- Choosing isolation above interactions.
- Loss of good feelings and a jaded approach to things that used to be enjoyed.
- Inability to focus.

- Sleep loss.
- Physical and mental fatigue.
- Avoiding management and exploration of emotional reactions.
- Nightmares.
- Hopelessness.
- Complaining easily.
- Overeating
- Self-medication with drugs or alcohol.
- Lack of self-care.
- Complaints about conduct or attitude in the workplace.
- Denial that there's a problem and struggling on.

Compassion fatigue can appear as depression, withdrawal and highly emotional behaviour, for example crying a lot or becoming emotionally volatile by wearing emotions close to the surface, which are easily triggered by seemingly small situations. Or it can present as lack of caring at all, anger, blaming the sufferer and being generally difficult to colleagues. Another example of compassion fatigue presenting this way is being rough and impatient with dogs in our care.

Regardless of how it manifests, compassion fatigue is indicative of suffering. It's also confusion because to care so much, whilst being frustrated or too emotional to fulfil a role that you love is hard to understand. Without help and understanding though, the condition will just get worse until there's no escaping from it. If you or someone you know is showing many of these symptoms I urge quick action and help, to prevent the onset or escalation of depression.

The good news is that we can build ourselves up to cope with the roles we so want to be able to do, by learning about and procuring personal resilience. To be resilient is to be able to cope with things without them affecting your personal wellness and health. Every single person (and dog in our care) can learn resilience, when we understand how.

Chapter Five
Resilience

"It's your reaction to adversity, not adversity itself that determines how your life's story will develop."
- Dieter F. Uchtdorf

If you have read my book Inspiring Resilience in Fearful and Reactive Dogs, you will already know that I love this topic. Whether human or dog is suffering; by being sensitive in a world that can be difficult and unkind, resilience can be learned as a skill and it will make the world an easier place to be in. By learning to be resilient now, you will just get stronger and stronger as you go through life.

Habits of Resilient People

Resilience is the ability not to break on the inside when the outside is battered by a storm from life itself. It doesn't mean that you bounce back, it means that you can adapt and re-orientate to changes whether in the moment or the entirety of your life. It can be strong, or you can have low resilience at any time of your life.

Imagine that you're a boat near a beach, the water is your natural resilience and there are rocks all around your anchor point. When your resilience is high that water gets higher, taking you further from the rocks. If your resilience is low, the water is low and occasionally you even scrape on the rocks, even when the lake is calm. A storm blows in and if your water is high, you bounce around on the waves, safely until the storm is over. Yet if your water is low, you bounce around on the rocks, until you can take no more and break into pieces.

Our current awareness of resilience includes three factors:

- Trait theory means that the individual is naturally resilient as a personality trait. This has been considered for a long time to be the case and would be the natural aspect of being able to cope. In my opinion few people are born totally resilient but with some, that they learn to strengthen along the way.
- The second theory of resilience is something we have already touched upon with attachment theory. It's considered that the earlier years define our ability to be resilient later on. This is called protection and offers

the idea that early nurturing creates a more resilient character.

- Theory number three, which is highly relevant to us, probably the most important factor in our "what are we going to do now" thinking; the growth of resilience as a learning process. As we pass through our lives, ideally we grow in resilience naturally. The more we experience loss, trauma and life's natural trials the more we should be able to cope with them. It's important though that we acknowledge mental illness in this process, and flawed thinking patterns associated with all sorts of ideas from the wild mind. Ideally we grow in resilience as we age, but most of the time we have to make a conscious decision to respond in that way.

Think about people that you know and ask yourself how they deal with life. Do they smile at troubles? Perhaps their emotions never dictate their actions or maybe they are the person that offers support to others without flailing themselves. I once worked with a dog trainer at a charity who found dogs hilarious. Whilst everyone was worrying and stressing about how their dogs would perform in front of a dragon-like manager in dreaded tests, this trainer smiled at the dogs because she saw the bigger picture – and she loved them. Her professional resilience was admirable, and she was the best trainer in the place.

How about you? How do you cope if plans suddenly change? Do you smile and carry on or does your day go downhill from there? Do you see change as an opportunity, or does it strike the fear of doom and dread into you?

Compassion fatigue will affect the ability to cope and be resilient to pressure. Whilst once we may have been highly resilient, a few years later after a year or two working in dog rescue, or with a particularly difficult team of peers we may be fatigued - and our personal resilience is lower than it's ever been.

The excellent news is though, resilience can be learned, not only by life's trials but during calm times too. Keeping the water high is the key to weathering the storm when it arrives.

People who are naturally resilient or have learned to be, will share a number of traits and life choices that help them to cope in the world. It's a good idea to look at the following list and consider how your own compares to it:

- Physical self-care.
- Self-esteem and self-belief.
- Social wellness.
- A support system.

- Emotional intelligence.
- Positivity based on realism.
- Adaptability.
- Pro-activity.
- A focus on solutions.

Your own life and how the above points fit into it may surprise you, their vastness may even overwhelm you. The important thing to remember here though, is what works for others may not work for you. For example, you may only spend time with one other person and that could be your entire support system. The above points are vital for your wellbeing, yet the choice of how and how much they fit into your life will be bespoke to you as an individual.

Becoming Resilient

Let's take a closer look at them and how you can make them work for you.

Physical Self-Care

Physical self-care and awareness seems low on the priority of many dog professionals. It's the fundamental basis of wellness though and should be a priority. The body and brain relies on certain care to maintain a sense of health and wellbeing.

On a biological basis the human body is cellular. Cells

need excellent nutrients to thrive and reproduce. Without cells there would not be tissues, organs and systems. So, without the right nutrients, we would literally not exist. The body is naturally resilient though and even with a lifetime of bad diet and general disregard, illness may not appear until middle age. This isn't a diet book though and I'm not going to give you advice on physical nutrition. If you're interested in that – which you really should be – I can highly recommend Dr Patrick Holford's book "How Not to Die", which is a work of genius.

The focus here is how physical self-care may affect your psychological health. The saying "you are what you eat" is accurate and most importantly, so is "you feel what you eat".

The brain needs three things to function properly and even with everyday living and the idea that our diet is not too bad, we can miss out on the crucial things for brain function and regeneration. This includes omissions that are likely to affect our mental health. The three things that you should consider a priority for brain health and wellbeing are diet, oxygen and stimulation.

Diet not only includes fresh, brain enhancing foods but must also consider the brain dulling food too. We should not only consider what we eat but when we eat. Providing the brain with oxygen through regular physical exercise gives brain cells what they need to thrive. Stimulation is learning new skills, building new neural pathways and enhancing natural neuroplasticity.

Social and Support

Humans need each other, we have evolved that way. Friends, peers, partners and family all support our wellbeing. Even if we have little contact with blood family, family of choice usually does the same job.

How is your own support network? Whether you have a network of one or dozens of friends really doesn't matter as long as it works for everyone involved. My primary support network is my husband and my dogs, whilst you may have a large extended family and thrive in big groups. Everyone needs someone and regardless of specifics, loneliness should be avoided as it's one of the biggest destroyers of wellbeing that we can encounter.

Loneliness has been linked with depression and addiction in many studies. A well-known trial on rats showed that single rats would choose water laced with cocaine if they were alone, but when they had the same choice, whilst living with other rats they went for plain water. Whilst we are more connected than ever before, via a process of online contact and expansive social media, loneliness is considered a problem bigger than it's ever been. It's linked to health issues such as heart disease, stroke and immune disease.

In a study that compared the recovery of cancer victims by placing them in two groups, one where social contact with a group was facilitated throughout treatments by having group support sessions and one with no group. The treatment that involved extra social support showed a quicker and higher rate of recovery than the second group.

Whilst a recent survey showed young adults as the loneliest group we must also acknowledge how difficult it is to make friends as an older adult. Many people spend years alone after the loss of a partner. Some live with animals which really make a difference to wellbeing at any stage of life.

Working as a canine professional or self-employed professional from home bypasses all the potential friendships that we could make through the shared experience of a job. Even the worst positions at the most harrowing workplaces lead to striking up true friendships and long term relationships. If you live alone and only meet clients, you may be missing a strong support network and be susceptible to compassion fatigue. This is particularly relevant because many dog guardians see us as their chance to offload and we end up taking all their dark energy and fear home with us. Some of the things I have been told when consulting on dog behaviour would make your toes curl, and I'm sure you have – or will encounter – similar things too.

The type of work that we do as dog professionals can be exhausting. Dog loss is something that affects all of us, even if it's not our dog and we haven't lost them first hand. We can often take on people's grief and in such large amounts that we simply have nowhere to put it. Friendships, family and fun put things into perspective. A bad day at work can become just that when there's something else at the end of it. But if it's all there is, it can become your entire life.

Having a support network is directly related to being part of a support network. To have friends you must also be a friend. There are people in the world who take more than they give, unable to see that they leave people feeling used and bruised. Usually these people have developed a self-protection habit that will eventually isolate them and often they can't see it.

As part of self-care, when someone is continually taking from you, you have to create and maintain a safe distance, most importantly remember that their behaviour is about them not you. True friendship is equal and even – sometimes it means supporting and sometimes it means being supported in return. When people can't offer support – for their own reasons – they usually find that when they need someone, they are all alone, which is very sad. We often see this type of behaviour in people that have addictions to either substances from outside themselves or beliefs and destructive patterns within.

Ask yourself now how much support you offer to others and whether they offer you the same amount back. Are your friendships (with your friends AND your family) conducive to your good health?

It can be easy to make friends on social media, because we can do it in our PJ's with our dogs. But instead of just being virtual, meet up in the real-world and do something fun. I do this a lot. Most of the time it's been a great success and we won't talk about the rest.

Self-Belief

We are inherently hard on ourselves. Dog people in particular struggle to focus on our strengths and we may even believe we don't actually have any, which is madness born of low self-belief. This part of your resilience toolkit is directly related to the wild mind we have already discussed and can benefit greatly from the practice of mindfulness. You may be visited regularly by the whispering voice telling you that you can't do it, you are not good enough or that everyone else is better than you.

Lack of self-belief comes directly from early learning. We are particularly tender young things for the first few years of our lives and we related everything that happens back to ourselves and what we were doing at the time. Being self-focussed (not selfish) is part of our learning and development on earth.

The self-focus of youth is totally natural and can be helpful or detrimental. We didn't know back then that one of our parents abandoned us because of their faults not ours. We were not aware that unhappiness in the adults around us was due not to us, but to other things. In extreme cases such as abuse, children feel like it's their fault and the abusive adult often reinforces that feeling to protect themselves. The result of taking responsibility for the bad things during childhood is that we become adults who we think cause bad things.

We can take responsibility for the bad stuff and learn that anything we do get right is nothing much to celebrate either, all based on early experiences. Something simple like emotional coolness and high expectations can cause low self-belief that whispers from the side lines of life forever.

Everyone's learning is different and an amalgamation of lessons we have discussed so far. If we could look at the life of one individual through a series of learning experiences, we might get a fair idea of how they cope, but there are so many variables that it wouldn't be detailed.

If we suffer with low self-belief we often give up on things easily. We might start a new hobby, buy a variety of tools, not get it right first time and sell everything on Ebay. We may not go for a promotion, avoid following our dreams or starting a diet and exercise regime, or a study path over and over again, only to stop a few days later, furthering our idea that we can't do anything useful at all.

There's something fascinating about beliefs, regardless of whether they are the beliefs we hold about ourselves, others or the world around us, The first belief we form is at risk of becoming our most powerful truth on the matter. So if we form strong beliefs about ourselves before we reach the age of seven, it not only becomes our truth, but we spend the rest of our lives gathering evidence to support that belief. If we don't learn something better and different from our first belief before we reach twenty years old, our first experience of that new knowledge is at risk of becoming our truth.

An excellent example of this is the widespread idea perpetuated in the media about dominance and dogs. Many peoples' first experience of dog training and behaviour is from watching TV. If they see a strong character perpetuating a myth, they will then believe that myth and start gathering their own evidence for it. The same person will then go around telling other people that the myth is in fact reality.

It's easy to understand the structure and reinforcement of beliefs through the example above. What about beliefs about ourselves though? They feel so real and what about if we take our mind off the idea that we are not capable? We might miss the truth – that everyone else thinks we were incapable after all. How much sense does that make to you? If it sounds just like a random, painful and cruel jab from the wild mind, that's because it is.

The fact of the matter is that you can do anything you want to do. That's not platitudes to make you feel better either, it's just facts. We can all do much to build our self-belief, taking ourselves from a place of challenge avoidance to success. We might need to build it from the ground up by setting up small steps that we can succeed in taking, embracing the success and moving along towards bigger goals, in bite sized manageable chunks. Perhaps you could start by finishing this book? By reading every book on your kindle that you haven't finished. By walking a mile before breakfast five days a week or taking an online course and actually finishing it. When you begin to finish the small tasks you have set yourself, you will soon be finishing larger ones without noticing how much bigger they are. An important thing to keep in mind if you tend to leave projects and ideas half-finished; the first step is to finish it. It can be tempting to think that you can't do a good job on something, so why bother finishing it at all. Why not choose a shiny new task and start again but get it perfect this time around? If you do that, stop! By restarting something new instead of finishing something you have already started, you are reinforcing the idea that you can't finish things. This becomes a habit quickly and then an opinion of yourself. It's also ammunition to the wild mind, and trust me he will use it.

So, choose something you have started and finish it. Then choose something else until you have finished at least 80% of those good ideas that you gave up on. Your self-belief will become strong, as you build new foundations and your achievements will raise the roof.

Optimism

We can redefine optimism as positivity with realistic expectation. Optimistic thoughts, feelings and expectations are sometimes innate but more often they must be created and nurtured to become default thinking. Remember the negative bias?

If we were lucky as children, our parents started to forge optimism into us directly after we were born. They set up our environment for excellent learning and parented us with grace, starting our natural optimism early in our lives. Or we may have been emotionally, physically or psychologically neglected and become pessimistic, expecting the worst outcome every step of the way. Most of us are somewhere in between.

People that are resilient practice optimism because it prevents worrying, fortune telling and projecting bad results into the future. It's actually better to have no expectation of a situation than expect the worst from it.

Pessimistic expectations can make life very difficult indeed, even when it doesn't need to be. For example, you may be attending a dog behaviour event where you have to meet and spend time with a lot of online friends that you haven't met before. As the event gets closer you may start to worry about it. You could start to worry about the motorway drive and expect danger and delays, worry about whether you will fit in with the people you know, or be certain you will make a show of yourself due to social anxiety.

You may really want to go to the event but it's outside your comfort zone so three days before you are left with a choice:

1. Do you expect a good journey and lovely time, making new friends and gathering bags of useful dog knowledge?
2. Or do you expect dangerous drivers, to get lost, to arrive late and that once everyone meets you they will see how dull you are and no longer want to know you?

Neither of the above things have happened. In fact, none of your expectations have come into any kind of form because they are not in this moment and never were. Yet if you were to start worrying about the conference two weeks before, your body's stress system is likely to be activated and you will experience physical changes. It could soon be that you are getting stressed whenever thoughts of the conference enter your mind, so you sell your ticket and get on with your life in the comfort zone.

Alternatively, you could take life one moment at a time and make yourself realise that your comfort zone is not the place to grow into your potential. So you go to the event, which you will enjoy because it's all about dogs and something you really wanted to do. Then next time you see something similar and decide to attend, it will be easier.

Forging optimism as an adult is hard, particularly if we have practiced worry for so long. Like any other practice it takes self-exploration and careful awareness of your thoughts, inclusive of the ability to recognise the wild mind, which would wrap you in cotton wool and never let you anywhere near the boundaries of your comfort zone.

Through study we are told that learning optimism is empowering. It is linked through testing to business success and even fewer injuries in sport, by the participants that practice optimism. People that practice optimism present it as a magic ingredient in their lives because everything they expect to go right usually does.

The most interesting thing about optimism and pessimism in our lives is that the same single experience can occur for two people yet their experience of it can be totally different. One will use it to further their resilience and self-belief whilst not even considering any negative connotations from it. The other may see it as yet another kick from this hardship called life, and not see any positivity in the experience at all. Most of us are somewhere in between.

It's an excellent idea to examine your thoughts when faced with a challenge. What is your natural go-to expectation of the challenge? Ask yourself why! An excellent side effect of growing self-belief through small self-set challenges is the growth of optimism alongside it.

Laughter and Humour

Laughter is the ultimate positive emotion. Related directly to happiness, humour is an important tool for personal well-being and resilience.

In various studies laughter has been proven to relieve pain by producing endorphins which are the body's pain relief chemical. It causes tension in the muscles, which then relax and stay more relaxed than before, for up to 24 hours. Laughter builds relationships, prevents loneliness, lowers blood pressure, releases mental and physical tension and heightens the immune response.

If you have been in a situation where laughter is trying to get out in response to something in the environment you will know that it is often uncontrollable. We can't laugh at something we don't find funny and we can't stop laughing at something we do. We actually don't know much about why we laugh, or the reasoning behind it, but we do know that it can affect the entire body, even the limbs and ability to breathe.

Scientists have found that laughter itself seems to be predominantly about people. It's a natural communication tool that enhances relationships with those around us. Laughter builds bonds.

Laughter and communication are generally always intertwined. Whether we create something that makes other people laugh, or we laugh with someone else, it's all about relationships with others. Laughter leads to bonding because it makes us feel good. It makes us want to return to the source of our amusement again and again, because it changes how we feel.

Humour begins as a natural behaviour and then becomes affected by learning experiences and life in general. As children we tend to play and laugh a lot. We enjoy everything and find even unpleasant things funny. As our personalities develop, so does our sense of humour. As we get older and develop the intelligence that shapes wisdom and a mature outlook, our humour becomes subtler. We begin to laugh at situations, or even life itself.

As adults we have often a sense of humour that has been learned from our local communities yet is not universally recognised. Whilst we consider some things funny inside of our own social circles, society rules or even geographical areas, they may not be funny outside of them. As adults we have often learned to laugh at the things that embarrass us, or the stressors that affect our lives. This varies with individuals, but it is generally a healthy attitude to take as opposed to rumination or even depression about life.

When mental health issues occur, we can forget how to laugh. Similarly, if we are always in our comfort zone, we get fewer chance of new experiences, which can lead to the good feeling associated with laughter.

Humour is part of resilience and optimism because it twists a bad situation happening to us, into something funny. Nothing has changed about the situation, but how we feel about the situation is much more beneficial to us. An important part of humour which some people have, is the ability to laugh at yourself which will give a much healthier perspective than worry because it helps to detract from the seriousness of any situation. Can you laugh at yourself? I imagine life may be difficult if you can't.

Here's an example of perspective from a situation that happened to me recently. I'm losing my hearing earlier than expected in my life. I also run an online business with my husband so when I'm waiting for appointments, I'm usually messing with my phone to catch up on the job. Yesterday I was in the waiting room at the dentist and heard my name called, so hopped up and went to the door. In the doorway I become entangled with another patient, called Barry. Poor Barry was the one actually called with no mention of Sally at all. When we were detangled, and Barry successfully went to his appointment, my first flush of embarrassment was replaced with a wave of despair. So, I changed the perspective there and then and have giggled about the situation ever since.

Hearing loss is serious business it can be isolating, embarrassing and depressing. I'm determined that for me it's going to be another reason to laugh and practice different perspectives, which is something any of us can do with any challenge that enters our lives.

Don't get me wrong, not every situation is funny. It can be hard to find humour during grief and crippling depression, but it's available as a resilience tool for most of our lives and provides the most beneficial physical and emotional results. Humour certainly shouldn't be overlooked.

The laughter type termed *gallows humour* began in Germany as *galgenhumor* and describes cynical humour or satire that we use to cope in difficult or traumatic situations. It is linked with resilience and hope and has the power to soothe suffering, producing mental and physical relaxation and relief in times of trouble. If you don't laugh often, it's time to laugh more because laughter therapy exists for one reason. It works!

Meaning

When we wake up in the morning and have a dozen

things to do before lunch it could be easy to believe that we would be happier with a lottery win, so we don't have to do anything. Part of our wellness though, is that our lives have meaning. So it's an excellent idea to ask yourself whether the things you choose to do in your life have real and valuable meaning to you and if they don't, perhaps it's time for a change.

Most people who work with dogs do so because they love them. In many ways, they give meaning to our lives. Dogs we live with greet us as we wake, we tend to their needs with devotion and spend time learning about them, so we can further understand and communicate with them. All of that gives us meaning.

Trials and tribulations also give us meaning. For example, if we lost a job, we have meaning to find another or start a business. It's common when we live with an ageing or sick dog to make them our meaning, we spend a lot of time caring for them and making sure their extra needs are met. Then when they leave us, we lose that sense of meaning along with the dog we love, so we suffer doubly.

If you take a different stance to the things that trouble you, for example you may have a client who is difficult, and you have to work extra hard with them, view them as your meaning. You will learn skills from them that easier clients don't trigger. Those skills will be with you forever and rather than viewing them with frustration or annoyance, consider them as part of your journey to satisfaction, through their unique ability to bring meaning into your life. When you finally succeed with the more difficult clients, you will have benefitted from them twice, because your accomplishment will also build your resilience, because succeeding at something always does.

Everyone has meaning, we are all vitally important to someone, even to our dogs and our unique skills are precious in the world. Ask yourself though, do you act with meaning and are the things you do on a daily basis aligned with your own values? Having a meaningful life is excellent for self-belief. Whether you volunteer for an hour a week, run an online auction for charity, do home checks for a rescue or do something different altogether – the more meaning you have that's aligned directly with your heart and values, the better your life will be.

Engagement

Are you always distracted? When did you last get into *the zone* with something? There's a human need to find engagement, it's excellent for the brain and wellbeing. We often talk about engagement with dogs as an amazing tool for learning and it really is.

Engagement is natural mindfulness and when we

experience it, there's nothing like it. People that are excellent at one skill, are so good at it because they become truly engaged in the activity and there's no room for anything else in their mind at that point.

Experiencing engagement seems to take you to another level, one that you can't feel when you're not in it, but you can get lost in when you are. For example, if you're a seasoned runner, you could get to the end of a five mile run and realise you only remembered the first and last mile, because you were totally in the zone and engaged for the middle three.

There are many ways to find engagement, one of the best in our industry is playing with your dog – or in fact anyone's dog. It's about being completely single minded in your activity and not distracted by anything outside of that moment. It's about unplugging from the world, which is something that we all need to do for complete peace of mind.

Engagement strengthens resilience, it makes you stronger within. Many runners say that they run because they need to. And that's because it gives them the resilience that helps with the rest of their lives. Dogs, knitting, running, writing, dancing, playing and many other activities trigger engagement and when you practice regularly your life will be wonderfully enhanced and you will be more resilient for it.

Being resilient is like a vaccination against compassion fatigue and if anyone needs that, dog professionals do. All of the points above, although they may seem unrelated to your professional life, they will be the framework that keeps you standing tall throughout tough times, when you need it most.

Chapter Six
People – The Ultimate Test

The woman who follows the crowd will usually go no further than the crowd. The woman who walks alone is likely to find herself in places no one has been before.
- Albert Einstein

For the first part of this chapter I'm going to address something that I believe to be highly important when we work with dogs as part of a team of people. It's important to realise that we can't change people and we actually shouldn't try. What we should and can do though – which is the only power we really have – is change how they make us feel and like everything else, that starts with understanding.

Humans are an extremely successful species. We are spreading across the world and using resources up like no species ever has before, no other animal can touch us and the more we learn the stronger we get. Through our endless strength; we have created an existence and lifestyle for ourselves that has made us vulnerable. The species is strong, but the individuals are needy and a little bit lost. In the distant past we were like free animals that spent time doing the basics. Food, reproduction and play were important and took up a lot of our time, but now food and reproduction are cheap and safe, a lot of us have forgotten to play.

Our physical needs are met, and physical danger rarely occurs but the body and brain may not have caught up yet; and it needs to put the stress response somewhere. So, it's moved over to social danger in a response that makes perfect sense.

Humans are a group animal. We have been so successful because we pulled together and pooled our resources, minds, ideas, strength and bodies. Social skills are at the centre of this existence, people that are socially excellent tend to get a lot of followers and friends.

The Nature of Defence

Imagine a few thousand years ago and a group of our ancestors still lived the simplest life possible. We joined a group and that group was strong. We pooled skill and resources, with excellent results. On the edge of the settlement predators waited for their dinner. Then imagine one awkward individual. She might not fit into the group, she might do something wrong and be cast beyond the settlement, straight into the lion's belly. Physical safety, even back then was linked directly to social safety. Now, where physical danger is much less prevalent; social safety has become our natural priority, because our bodies and brains haven't caught up with the speedy evolution of our lives as they are now.

Let's go back to the group before we carry on moving forward and pay some more attention to the sinister aspect of laughter. Whilst it's been studied and considered in great detail, we don't know for certain why humans laugh but we do know it's good for us – unless you're being laughed at. One of the most common theories presents the idea that humans laugh to communicate their superiority.

This starts early, with teasing between children and escalates through school life and for some people it never stops. Within this theory and in our group of early humans, social isolation and laughter could meet to become physical isolation.

In the world as it is today, social isolation is either a choice or forced upon us. As we are generally physically safe, isolating someone socially is the modern-day equivalent of isolating them physically and sending them out into the world alone. If you have ever been laughed at by a group of people you will know how this feels and believe me, it's pretty awful.

So why do people do it to each other?

We are complicated, kind, unkind, conscious and unconscious animals. We are all different and have all learned different things during our time in the world. From the moment we were born, we were learning. If we were nurtured as we grew, we learned that we were safe, but a neglected baby learns not to trust. A we get older and peers take the place of our immediate family, we learn even more about others and how they operate. From our early family and the early experiences we have with our peers, we decide our own fears and how we are going to act towards others.

If we feel secure as we grow, learn trust and to be compassionate we become an empathetic person and that dictates how we act towards others and in a group. If our early years are fraught with unkindness and perceived danger, we seek social and emotional safety. It's not black and white though, we can learn empathy in some situations and unkindness in others. People can learn in such a way that they would lay down their life for their own family but carry out severe racist attacks on people from other parts of the world.

When we work with dogs we usually also have to work with people. Some of the worst times I have had in a workplace were within my role at a national animal charity packed with cliques and bullies. Another charity I worked at was very different; the team were wonderful, kind and pulled together, but the manager was extremely insecure, therefore very difficult indeed.

I would go so far as to say that the fear of social isolation is the fundamental reason for all nasty deeds towards other people. The less enlightened a person has become during their time on this earth, the more they will strive to stay safe within a group whilst working hard to isolate others. This is how bullies work, why a group of people turn their back on one individual and why people encourage others to laugh at the quiet, different and humble individual in a group.

Enlightenment changes things. When we become enlightened, we realise that it doesn't matter whether we are in a group or not. We don't mind being alone and often we embrace it. In addition, we learn to recognise that the bullies are fearful and way more lost than anyone else, even if they stand firm and loud, right at the centre of a group.

If you have been bullied or isolated through sharing beliefs or values, take heart that you are not alone. We are all alone together, and it's great. Remember that when someone hurts you, they are the centre of their pain, they are the victim of their own lack of enlightenment and you don't need to do anything but walk away from them and take care of yourself. Or if you feel strong enough, do that then use your strength to neutralise their treatment of the next victim too.

We all send out ripples into the world. The enlightened choice is to focus only on our own because the stronger your presence, the less you will be affected by others.

Realistic Expectations

> *"Never idealize others. They will never*
> *live up to your expectations"*
> - Leo Buscaglia

An important lesson to learn in life is that we are all different. If you expect people to hold the same values, manners and thoughtfulness as you do then you will probably be heartily disappointed. An excellent example of this is behaviour in crowds. Some people are continually thoughtful of others, their behaviour shows respect for the personal space of people around them. Other people appear rude, pushing and completely disregarding of anyone they share the space with.

If you were raised to be thoughtful and kind towards everyone you meet, people that were not raised that way could easily drive you crazy. You may find general respect of vast importance in your life on earth yet without accepting that other people don't, you could always be frustrated and angry by the behaviour of people you encounter.

Yes, it would be wonderful if everyone was thoughtful and empathetic, but many people haven't learned to be and unless we accept that and make peace with it, it can easily drive us crazy. To expect everyone to hold the same values as ourselves, sets them and us up to fail.

Try relaxing into life and having no expectations of anyone; you will have a very different experience in the world.

Not Everyone Will Like You

Another feeling left over from the evolution of safety in numbers is the idea that everyone must like you. It's not going to happen, and you might as well accept it. Being liked by everyone is pretty much impossible. You can be the nicest, most agreeable person and put yourself out over and over again for one particularly difficult individual and they will still forge a dislike for you because of something going on in their own head.

It can be easy to blame yourself and ask yourself over and over again what you could have done differently, what you have done to deserve their behaviour towards you; you might even take responsibility for their actions – particularly if you suffer with low self-esteem. If their dislike of you goes beyond any ability to communicate and heal the rift, it can be easy to get angry, drowning in the unfairness of their behaviour and why they should not be allowed to get away with it. Neither of these responses will help or empower you.

The only thing that will empower you is the knowledge that it's not their behaviour that makes you feel bad, but how you feel about their behaviour. When we confirm that our feelings are directly related to how we think, we are empowered, because we don't have to listen to our thoughts and certainly don't have to let them change how we feel.

Taking responsibility for how we feel is the biggest power that we have in this life on earth. The knowledge brings peace of mind, alleviates needless suffering and makes us far less susceptible to the damaging addiction that we call blame.

The Blame Game

Blame is addictive and disempowering. You probably know someone who blames everyone else for their life, a situation or the state of the world. To blame is to put the responsibility on someone else for a specific occurrence; sometimes people are to blame for something bad that happens, and the responsibility is indeed theirs. Sometimes though, people use blame to avoid their own responsibility in a situation or even in their entire lives and this is a highly destructive habit.

Even when someone else is to blame for something; they may have wronged you quite badly and affected you seriously, allowing them into your very existence disempowers you. Try to consider your life from two perspectives for a moment here and ask yourself:

1. Do you create your experience of the world from within yourself?
2. Are you victim to the world from outside yourself?

Whether you choose to see your life as part of the model I use, or you choose to take a completely scientific view, these points apply to you. There's one important thing to keep at the centre of your world at all times, only you control how you feel. So, you may be really hurt by someone and feel angry towards them, they may well have been a complete ratbag to you, but they are not inside you and they can't make you feel something. It's not what they do that's the problem, it's what you feel about what they do that will make your life hard.

When you realise this, your entire perspective will

change because with practice, you will become totally empowered by knowledge of the fact that you create your experience of the world from within and no-one can affect you from the outside. With this viewpoint, you realise that blame is a pointless exercise, packed with unnecessary distress for yourself.

Emotional Intelligence.

Daniel Goleman introduces us to his work and knowledge of the term emotional intelligence, which has been labelled EQ. Goleman has studied Emotional Intelligence over many years and his book of the same name has more than 5,000,000 copies in print worldwide in 40 languages, and has been a best seller in many countries. EQ is directly associated with interpersonal and intrapersonal intelligence which is the capability to understand our own emotions and the emotions of others.

Emotional intelligence is explained by Goleman through a mind model based in biology. He describes it as;

- The thinking mind.
- The feeling mind.

In Steve Peter's model described in The Chimp Paradox, the feeling mind is equal to the chimp. So far in this book we have called it the wild mind. The biological basis is that the feeling mind is the most ancient part of the human brain, driven by the amygdala and limbic system. The younger part of the brain associated with logic and control over emotions, is the thinking mind. The amygdala which is involved in emotional responses is named the emotional hijacker of the brain, by Goleman.

This relatively small area of the brain has great power over us because of its ability to create instantaneous powerful emotional reactions that hijack our logic and even our power of choice. When we can't manage our emotional responses, they change how we think. When we can't manage how we think we lose control of how we feel and act. This loss of control can have a catastrophic effect on our lives, relationships, well-being and mental health. We can counteract its devastating effects by learning and practicing effective emotional intelligence.

In its entirety, emotional intelligence consists of four areas:

1. Awareness of our own emotions.
2. Motivation and regulation of our own emotional responses.
3. Empathy with others.
4. Awareness of the emotional responses of others in social and professional situations.

Awareness, motivation and regulation of our emotions grows with practicing mindfulness and empowerment through self-understanding, a topic that we have spent a lot of time on so far in the book.

There are two exercises I would like to share with you here to aid your own self-awareness of the emotional responses you may have to deal with in the course of your day. They bring you into the moment, as mindfulness does, but they focus this time on awareness of your own emotions. They can easily be remembered via the acronyms RAIN and STOP. Both or either of them can be applied when you experience a strong or distressing emotional reaction. Yet you can use them regularly for all types of emotion to grow your own emotional self-awareness, your EQ and general emotional resilience.

RAIN

1. **Recognition** of the emotion itself. Rather than trying to quell an emotion to prevent it changing how you feel, take a mental step back and examine it until you recognise exactly what that emotion is.
2. **Allow** the emotion to just be present for a little while. When you stop fighting it, it starts to lose power over you there and then.
3. **Investigate** within yourself what in your current environment triggered that specific

emotion and why. It can be a tenacious link to something bad that happened once, or fear that someone might not like you. Investigation is the second step of eliminating the strength of the emotion and its power over you. It's thought that 80% of our negative emotions are based on past experiences and only 20% are based in the present or anxiety about the future. If we consider that there is only this moment, it doesn't make much sense to allow this emotion to upset you, does it?

4. **Non-identification** is the final blow to what was once a potential hijack. Just like we assume the wild mind is a separate part of us, we realise that the emotions triggered by that same wild thinking is separate from us too.

Just as the model we call RAIN can help you to identify emotions as they arise, the model called STOP can prevent emotional hijack, if you apply it swiftly and with care. The process called STOP is a structured moment of mindful awareness that brings you back from the brink of emotional hijack and balances your body and mind, all in a moment or two.

This is great for nervousness, a flash of annoyance or if you experience an influx of empathy which leads to personal distress for you;

1. **Stop** what you're doing.
2. **Take** ten counted, deep breaths and focus on the breath as it enters and leaves your body.
3. **Observe** your thoughts and if they have affected how you feel, be aware of that too.
4. **Proceed** by rerouting your path to one that is mindful and not an emotional knee-jerk reaction.

Try to consider your thinking mind and the wild mind as two parts of an entire mind, that you live with on this dance through life. The ability to think clearly gives us clarity and realism. The ability to draw from the feeling mind gives us helpful emotions in the right circumstances. A mind that only consisted of one part of these two would only give us half of the colourful lives that we are lucky enough to live. Our task is to understand them as a team and learn to live with them, getting the best from each, to our ultimate success.

Connection

> *"Communication - the human connection*
> *- is the key to personal and career success"*
> - Paul J. Meyer

Whilst most of us can talk and listen there are few great communicators. We can recognise the excellent communicator by how easily others are drawn to them. Excellent communicators often have natural empathy and are high on the charisma scale, people generally like them. Communication skills are a vital part of not only emotional intelligence but also of everyday life and are usually twinned with highly effective emotional intelligence.

A good communicator sees not only what they need to say but how it may make the receiver of the message feel. Just as they are aware of their own emotions, they can empathise with the emotions of others. Communication involves more than passing across words to someone else. Excellent communication involves listening, looking, body language and general assessment of the other party in the communication loop.

Listening

Good listening includes the ability to stop talking. When we meet dog guardians who we need to obtain information from, we need to establish rapport with them initially, then guide them towards giving us the right information. We must also curb the tendency that people have, of straying into irrelevant facts and opinions. This is actually a difficult task for all types of dog professional regardless of your exact role. Dog trainers, coaches, behaviourists, veterinary staff and rescuers are the most vulnerable to it though. When people have dealt with situations that have tested them to the point of their own emotional upheaval they tend to offload.

If you are naturally high in empathy you are likely to have experienced this a lot. If your empathy type is naturally emotional, you may have experienced much personal distress from others offloading on you. This is a great reason to keep working on your resilience.

When people talk without giving pause it's hard work for the listener. When we use emotional intelligence within communication, we don't fall into the trap of becoming an incessant talker, instead we become a skilled and interested listener that can guide the speaker, whilst getting the information we need. Part of excellent listening is careful observation, clarification by questions, guidance through prompts and the ability to curb excessive talking without upsetting the speaker. Excellent communicators are also aware of (and avoid) listening blocks such as the ones below:

- Always needing to be right is an active block to listening.
- Assuming you can read the speakers mind because you have some experience with what they are telling you is a block to effective listening.

- Comparing people to others who may or may not be part of the communication.
- Daydreaming whilst someone is talking.
- Derailing is the act of quickly changing the subject if a topic becomes uncomfortable or not interesting enough.
- Filtering information to make it match what you already might think is the case, which can result in missing out important points.
- Identifying with the speaker by making their experience match one you have also experienced, therefore believing you know exactly the thing they are telling you, before they even say it.
- Making the mistake of judging someone based on their appearance or the way they speak can close your ears and eyes to their message.
- Offering advice before the speaker has given you their full message is counter-productive.
- Placating and trying to be nice can take your mind away from the message being given to you, because you are so worried about how well you're being perceived.
- Rehearsing is the act of preparing what you are going to say next, rather than listening to what is still being said.

When we are new to canine coaching or behaviour

consultations it can be easy to spend those first few encounters worrying about how your client perceives you. Mindfulness will help with that and try to practice focus on the information you need and the dog knowledge that you have, rather than the general strain that can be caused by low self-belief and lack of experience.

Communicating Your Requirements

Using the word "I" is an excellent way to communicate what you need from someone. Rather than saying, "you need to tell me exactly what happened when your dog bit you" which can be interpreted as a command to a distressed dog guardian, simply replace the first word "you" with "I". Remembering that when someone is distressed about something, they are likely to be at risk of emotional hijack and anything that could be interpreted as blame or telling them what you do may cause emotional distress and be counter-productive.

"I would like you to give me as much detail as you remember about what happened when your dog bit you" is far less likely to incite negative emotional response, because it's about you and what you need rather than linked to something they are doing – therefore people tend to respect that much more. Try using the approach in your everyday language when communicating with people and see how much difference it makes in their responses.

Conflict Resolution

Conflict is something that everyone has to deal with at some point. Most of the time though, it's based in lack of effective communication. Because we humans are not mind readers, we project how we think people feel and then base our own behaviour on that, so it's easy to create conflict where there need not be any.

Don't get me wrong, there are some situations where it's unavoidable. People tend to fit into certain archetypes and some are more difficult than others. Archetypes just means the presence of our personality and some personalities seem to like drama. There are also incidents where emotional hijack happens well before we have the chance to assess how we are reacting. Professionally though, conflict of any type should be dealt with quickly, assertively and without escalation.

Being assertive simply means that you communicate without emotion. Guarding your language and emotional responses will help you to cope with the emotional responses of someone else. By staying calm and trying to reach a mutual understanding, the person you are talking to is likely to entrain to your communication style. Consider it this way, your true minds are present but so is your wild mind and the other person's wild mind too. Imagine that there's not only a conflict between you and the other person but a conflict between both of your wild minds, which are battling to dictate how each of you behave. Their wild mind might get a low blow in, which prompts your own to retaliate – now you have a choice, you can soothe the furious wild animal in you and respond through the reasonable and assertive one. The other option is allowing an emotional hijacking, where the situation goes way beyond everyone's control, usually resulting in regrets and battles that are never resolved.

Within conflict, we also have to consider the ego of the wild mind. He likes to be heard, he has a tendency to get carried away with his self-image and this can dictate how he acts and react too. Ego is proud, it won't apologise or go back on what's it's decided. Egotistical thinking is the reason people won't change incorrect opinions, why they won't ask for help and why people fall out with those they love – sometimes for years at a time. We can't stop the ego and we can't eliminate the wild mind - and neither should we - because they bring us self-esteem, happiness, love and self-belief too. WE just have to learn to compromise with them and achieve the best of both worlds.

People tend to tell others, anyone that will listen, if they have a bad experience with a service or person. It's even worse nowadays because they can splash it all over social media too. If you do encounter someone who does that kind of thing, don't fret. Just be assertive, live by your conscience and don't get involved in any kind of battle.

Chapter Seven
Your Professional Presence

"I believe in professionalism, but playing is not like a job. You have to be grateful to have the opportunity to play"
- Wynton Marsalis

Professional presence is the foundation of successful business and the respect of your name in the dog world. Think for a moment about a true professional that you know. Pick out five of their traits that you admire, that you believe makes them so excellent. They may be private, friendly, have excellent emotional intelligence, be a fantastic communicator or be able to share their knowledge in a way that helps you to understand it perfectly.

Your own growth is based on how you are perceived by others, both your clients and those in your industry.

The Internet

The internet is a place packed with potential. Your

online presence can work for or against you, depending how well you use it. It's a great tool if you use it wisely.

Your Website

If you're a canine professional who shies away from the internet but wants to grow your business, it's well worth getting to know the online world because used carefully, it's excellent for growing a business. Know though, that a bad website will put people off your services.

Luckily many of the self-designed websites available today are easy to use. If you can't do it yourself or don't have an eye for design it's really worth getting some skilled help - it's better than putting a sorry looking website. Not all of us have an eye for design; anything I have ever created tends to look much like a primary school project.

Something fantastic about the internet is that people can make their own brand, and many do. Artists, photographers and even the guardians of especially cute dogs, can grow their following to millions if they get the engagement right. An audience growing quietly in the background could lead you directly to an excellent idea later.

A blog is a good idea! Regardless of your actual

profession within the dog world, you can use a blog to grow a following and to help people with their dogs. Be careful about the general nature of your blog too, keep it helpful and positive. Whilst the inflammatory posts generally get a lot of feedback, much of it is based on negativity. Negative feedback, bad comments and generally having strangers call you names, is not fun so keep that in mind when you write your posts. It's also a good idea to put them through spell and grammar checks before uploading too as there's always someone that gets hung up on grammar and feels good about shouting an error from the rooftops.

If writing is a dream for you, there is really nothing to stop you from doing it. I left school with no qualifications and my writing was shocking. There were literally no sentences, it was all just one huge paragraph after another. After adulthood struck I decided to get educated for the real world and my writing improved greatly, but it took time and effort. If you have a message and can put it out into the world via the written word, the grammar can be learned.

Social Media

Social media is a huge part of our lives nowadays and how we conduct ourselves on there determines who people think we are. It's an odd situation that has never been part of the human experience until the most recent generations.

Social media is unique as we can think something in the safety of our living rooms, without fully thinking it through, and splash it out to hundreds of people at the touch of a button. This is great if we can mind our words before putting them into the world because it grows a professional following. However, if we are emotionally volatile and can't censor, we can easily fall into the trap of showing everyone we know our current emotional hijacking.

Using social media to benefit you and get your professional reputation and personality into the world is beneficial. It's free advertising and a great way to showcase products and services. I know a few people who have never advertised their business at all other than creating a Facebook page and providing an excellent service. Their reputation and Facebook page is enough to keep them in full time work, providing the service they have chosen to offer.

As it's such a huge part of our lives now, many of us have an online personality – an archetype based on how open we are and what we think is acceptable to show to others. It's important that your own archetype is as professional as possible, because you really don't know who is watching your activities.

Think about how you see others in the industry through their online personality. How do you feel when people rant about other professionals? What do you think of inflammatory comments and why? You may respect someone's work, but want to avoid meeting them at all costs because they complain a lot, appearing judgemental and petty online. Or you might be wonderfully taken by someone who is professional, kind and an excellent online communicator, a true professional. Ask yourself which you would like to be as your online following grows, then be sure that your actions reflect your answer.

If you use social media a lot, I suggest keeping your own page private and creating a second page for your professional persona. Choose your private friends carefully and network for business through your professional profile. It's a good idea to keep them separate if possible, and be as private about your life as you can.

For any professional page attached to your product or services, I also suggest that you police it carefully and steer well clear of any debatable topics that may cause friction or arguments because they will most certainly be associated with your professional personality. People will judge you on them. I oversee a couple of big pages and swipe away any negativity as soon as it appears, because online and in the physical world a negative opinion can spread easily, and gain momentum enough to become associated with you, your brand and your professional personality.

A Facebook page is a useful tool even for the most phobic of internet newcomers, because it talks you through a few simple steps then you can simply share things, and carefully include your services and products in some of your posts. Don't bash people to death with your name, offerings or products though, as that will put visitors off.

We recently had a new and excellent dog sitter staying with our four dogs and she uses her professional Facebook page to showcase the dogs in her care. So, from holiday we got to see our happy, relaxed and playful dogs every single day, often more than once. I believe her total devotion to dogs, plus the knowledge that people worry about their dogs when away, is the reason that our wonderful dog sitter is fully booked many months in advance. Think about what you can offer to clients and potential clients that gives them excellent value for the service you provide. There are so many options and remember, one excellent idea that you run with might just be the thing that changes your life completely.

Online Arguments

Online arguments can become extremely heated.

When you consider it through the lens of mind management we have covered, the online argument consists of emotional hijacking all over the world. The energy associated with fury towards strangers, based on words on a screen is pointless. If you're tempted to get involved in a row online, switch off and do something else instead – because no-one wins these things and the energy involved with them is dark and damaging.

Social media is an amazing opportunity; use it wisely and to your best possible benefit. In the wise words of activist and comedienne Franchesca Ramsey:

"The Internet is part of my job, so I have to approach it with a level of professionalism. I don't necessarily think it's changed who I am, but if anything, it's impacted the opportunities that have come into my life and the people that I've been able to develop relationships with - which I'm very fortunate and thankful for".

If you take the good bits from the internet and leave the rest, you will benefit greatly.

Whilst we may be told to dress smart, stand up straight and be efficient as a professional. The most important things in my opinion are to be nice but not soft, practice emotional intelligence in all communications, manage our minds and invest time in truly understanding dogs along with their people.

Continued Professional Development

Dog knowledge is integral to canine professionalism. It's really not enough to love dogs, we have to know what they are saying to us and be able to communicate back to them in a way they understand.

At risk of criticism here I'm going to say that no-one really knows dogs, other than the dogs. In addition, we can understand one dog, but not another. We must keep learning throughout our lives and choose our sources of information carefully.

Whether you studied dogs straight from formal education or have taken a career change later on really makes little difference. You may have a base education from school or college, yet the knowledge of our dogs is changing so much every year that topping up your professional development is of paramount importance.

Domestic dogs are a unique study opportunity for ethnologists. We can study the animal who is not human, in their natural environment which is domestication. We don't have to travel beyond our borders like we would if we were studying wild wolves. Thousands of years of evolution have bought the study subject directly onto our sofas. Whilst we can't be certain how they feel, dogs seem happy to live with us in the most part and we are certainly happy to live with them.

If you have never formally studied dogs before now, it's a great time to be doing it. Science loves them at the moment and new studies and theories are released every day. The options of study are vast too, but it's important to choose carefully.

Dog training and behaviour as a profession is currently self-regulated. Because of this, methods are varied, and education is a mixed bag. The theory that dogs are wolves still has a vast hold on the dog training and so does force and punishment. Methods are changing though, in line with science and eventually regulation is likely to come into force for dog trainers. Hopefully, it will be organised and based on proper learning theory and understanding of how damaging force and punishment is to dogs. Eventually the truth about outdated pack theory will surely be eliminated by proper education too.

To continue an efficient professional development, it's a good idea to split your learning between theoretical and practical education, on a regular basis. Home study is an excellent choice, which can be supplemented by practical workshops or volunteering on a practical basis somewhere – maybe in your everyday job if you're already a canine professional.

Be savvy about the market. There are a lot of course

providers with lots of promises out there. Dig deep with your research, find out what methods are taught and remember that if the methods are outdated, that particular education will soon be useless to you.

There is also a culture of creating membership organisations with expensive yearly fees, which provide only the name and a website badge yet cost as much as two or three excellent books would. If you're considering a course, ask lots of questions and if the answers are not completely clear to you, ask yourself why. Remember that all courses are self-regulated so if a membership organisation place is offered on the condition that you buy a specific course, ask yourself why that might be. If you're considering a membership organisation, ask what it offers in return for your cash and whether your money could be spent elsewhere to further your actual knowledge and education instead. When we work with dogs, it's vital to keep educated and up to date. But be wise with it too and don't just jump into the first option you find.

Making it Pay

The topic of income is directly linked to self-worth, money and that awkwardness people seem to have around it. There's an odd culture that's common within the dog based profession too, that people should give their advice away for free.

When one person asks for advice they only see their own question and think it's not much at all. Yet when you become the expert dog person, that one person becomes ten or twenty. I often get Facebook messages that barely acknowledge me, but dive straight into an abrupt request for dog advice. It drives me a bit mad, I'm sure it does you too if you are frequently in that position.

Studying dogs is a profession like any other, it takes care, money, time and effort which really needs to be reflected in your income. Don't sell yourself short at any point and be sure to charge what you're worth for consultations and care. Be sure that your prices relate directly to your quality of service though, or your business won't work out in the long term.

The secret of making your job pay well and staying ethical is to understand how money works in people's minds. There's a strange culture around cash and something you can tap into if you do it right. Here's how to make your business pay:

1. Ensure you are offering top quality service by keeping up to date with your education and practicing professionalism at all times.
2. Always offer more value than you ask people to pay for. This is an important one, people will pay £1000 or £100 for the same thing. They may be different people and their

experience of the thing they buy will be different too – however – the value of what they are paying for can be exactly the same. I urge you to listen to your own inner voice with this and ask yourself in good conscience, whether the price you set for something offers your clients more value than they pay for.

3. There's more to costing than how much hard cash you can get from people, there's also ethics and energy. If your prices are higher than the trade you make for the money, then your business ethic needs tweaking, for it to be a real, ethical success.

4. If you offer a stellar service or an amazing product, don't be afraid to charge for it. Take some time and be honest with yourself. If you stick to the rule of keeping service or product value above cash value, your income will grow without a doubt, no matter what you decide to charge.

It's also a good idea to check out the value of things in your area. If I were to charge London prices in the North of England where I live now, the Cumbrians would probably lose their minds and I would get very few clients, if any at all.

Income Types

There are a number of income types available to you

as a good, canine professional. You could work in a traditional job, for a charity or other organisation, earning a wage or salary based on time worked. This leads to an income from a single source and is often considered the stable option.

You could work in a business of your own, on a self-employed basis. Self-employment gives you the option to have income from different clients. In our society today, this is considered a risk, particularly at the beginning. In reality, the more clients that you have, the less likely losing one will affect your overall income.

The above two income types involve swapping time for money.

Then there's passive income, which has gained a huge boost since the internet arrived. A business can be part or full time passive, depending on the nature of your role within it. I, for example, have a business that provides courses for students; in part it's passive because the same course is provided to many students. In part it's active because I tutor for the business and put continual effort in to maintain the experience and education welfare of the students. I also write books which I self-publish through Amazon, which provides a passive income too, but takes work to maintain and market.

I highly recommend that you consider getting yourself a full or part passive income stream. Every single person has a skill that they can offer to the world. Even if you work full time as a canine coach or behaviour consultant, you have a skill which you can use to create another income stream. If you can't think of anything, practice mindfulness and watch out for that idea to come passing through your quietened mind, then run with it.

Your Ultimate Success

We have covered a lot in quite a short book and I hope you have benefited from and enjoyed the process. The main lesson I really want you to take away from all of it, is that wherever your mind goes your life will follow.

It's a small statement but a huge lesson that has taken me many years to learn – gathering evidence along the way. You don't have to believe in a God, a subjective reality or a model like mine, to succeed. You do have to believe in yourself though, and by managing your mind with care and self-compassion you will reach your full potential, I promise you this.

Practice mindfulness at every opportunity; when you become mindful your unique and wonderful abilities will bubble to the surface of your life on earth. Grab opportunities, get outside your comfort zone and keep investing in your personal and professional growth. This time next year you can be living the life that so far has only been part of your dreams, you just have to go there in your mind first.

Final Note

If you're reading this through Kindle, could you please click the star rating at the end of the book? If you have the book in paperback would you please consider leaving a review on Amazon? Reviews and ratings are the lifeblood of self-published authors.

Reviews dictate readers and get my work seen by as many people as possible, so I would really appreciate it if you took a moment just to click to share your experience. Thank you.

If you have any questions or just want to say hello, you can contact me at my website sallygutteridge.com or email me at info@sallygutteridge.com. I respond to every single message.

Thank you for joining me.

Printed by Amazon Italia Logistica S.r.l.
Torrazza Piemonte (TO), Italy